March 30/1

Pete, My friend and colleague...

a modest book about a major

issue affecting our country

today. Fondly, Mark Malloch

CLOSING AMERICA'S JOB GAP

How to Grow Companies and Land Good Jobs
in the Age of Innovation

CLOSING AMERICA'S JOB GAP

How to Grow Companies and Land Good Jobs
in the Age of Innovation

Mary Walshok, Tapan Munroe & Henry DeVries

W Business Books

an imprint of New Win Publishing
a division of Academic Learning Company, LLC

Copyright © 2011 by University of California Regents
Published by WBusiness Books,
an imprint of New Win Publishing,
a division of Academic Learning Company, LLC
9682 Telstar Ave. Suite 110, El Monte, CA 91731
www.WBusinessBooks.com

Cover Design by Diego Torres

ISBN 10: 0-8329-0000-1
ISBN 13: 978-0-8329-0000-6

Printed in the United States of America
First Edition
15 14 13 12 11   1 2 3 4 5

Library of Congress Cataloging-in-Publication Data

Walshok, Mary Lindenstein.

Closing America's job gap : how to grow companies and land good jobs in the age of innovation /
by Mary Walshok, Tapan Munroe, Henry DeVries.

   p. cm.

Includes bibliographical references.

ISBN 978-0-8329-0000-6

1. Labor market--United States. 2. Job creation--United States. 3. Occupations--United States. 4.
Vocational guidance--United States. 5. Employment forecasting--United States. I. Munroe, Tapan.
II. DeVries, Henry. III. Title.

HD5724.W263 2010

331.10973--dc22

2010048017

CONTENTS

FOREWORD

Have you ever heard an alarm bell go off in a hotel? What did you do? You probably ignored it and assumed that in a matter of minutes the alarm would be turned off, the manager would apologize over the loudspeaker, and life would go on.

That's exactly what Garry Ridge, president and CEO of WD-40 Company, did a few years ago on a cold evening in London. But in his case the irritating alarm bell continued to sound, interfering with Garry's plan to relax that night and watch a British comedy in his room. What finally got Garry's attention was the security guard banging on the door and insisting that everyone evacuate. Not having time to dress warmly, Garry was directed down a flight of stairs and ushered to an open park near the hotel as it started to rain. He remained in the park for over an hour, cold and wet, as a bomb scare was checked out.

Knowing Garry as I do from coauthoring our book, *Helping People Win at Work*, I know he views everything as a learning opportunity and so do his tribe members at WD-40 Company. On his flight home to California a few days after the incident, Garry began to reflect on his trip and how stupid it had been to ignore the initial alarm bell. He quickly realized that alarm bells have a purpose—especially if we choose to hear them and act on them.

Do you have any alarm bells going off in your life, either professionally or personally, that you are choosing to ignore or that the busyness of your life is drowning out? If so, you might want to think twice and take action before negative consequences sneak up on you and have a major impact on what you are doing.

Why did I spend so much time discussing alarm bells? Because this book, *Closing America's Job Gap: How to Grow Companies and Land Good Jobs in the Age of Innovation*, is all about a big alarm bell. While the economy is beginning to turn, the job market is lagging behind. While in the past we have looked to large industrial companies for job creation, the real job opportunities today are being created by smaller innovative entrepreneurial ventures. However, today's workforce does not have the ready skills to fill these jobs. The concern is that policy-makers in Washington, business leaders, and individuals trying to navigate this very difficult period of American history are not paying attention to the lack of alignment that exists between our innovation and business-development sector and our workforce- and talent-development sector.

The authors—Mary Walshok, a thought leader and subject-matter expert on employability, career innovation, and the new innovation economy; Tapan Munroe, a recognized author, speaker, consultant, and advisor in economics; and Henry DeVries, a job and career expert—suggest this is a fixable problem requiring a change in mindset among individual workers in terms of realizing what Peter Drucker told us years ago: "All work is learning." It is fixable if employers will put a little more time and money into continuous learning in the workplace. It is fixable if the government reexamines its current workforce education and training strategies and reengineers them to fit the demands of the twenty-first-century global economy. To do this, we have to stop falling asleep at the switch in America and take action in response to this alarm bell.

Thanks, Mary, Tapan, and Henry, for sounding the alarm. Let's hope that policy-makers, business leaders, and individuals trying to survive in this tough economic time will listen. It's all about empowering our workforce. It cannot be done alone by any of these three groups; *together* we must devote energy to solving this problem and closing America's job gap.

Ken Blanchard,
Coauthor of *The One Minute Manager*® and *Leading at a Higher Level*

PREFACE:

Ringing the Alarm Bell on Jobs

This was not the book we intended to write. While writing a book on innovation and job creation, the three authors began comparing notes and uncovered an alarming situation. Mary, a sociologist studying the workforce, saw the trends through her work with the U.S. Department of Labor. Tapan, an economist studying innovation in Silicon Valley and other high-tech areas, was alarmed by the data coming from sources such as the Bureau of Labor Statistics. Henry, a journalist reporting on jobs and careers, picked up similar disturbing threads as he interviewed unemployed and underemployed Americans. Articles in *The Economist* and the *New York Times* shed further light on a disturbing forecast.

Together, the authors agreed that the message "invest in innovation to create good jobs" is not good enough. There is a growing disparity between the good jobs being created by innovation in the United States and the availability of American workers with the skills to fill these good jobs. Unless Americans are alerted to the growing job gap, the dream of good jobs for all is unlikely to be realized. Like volunteers sounding the alarm bell, the authors of this book are calling upon employers, job-seekers, entrepreneurs, and policy-makers, especially at the state and county level, to take a hard look at what is really shaping the labor market today.

While there are many books for job-seekers and countless others on growing innovative companies, this book is written for both employers and employees because their futures are inseparably intertwined. The main message of our book became this: To ensure competitive companies and rewarding careers in the age of innovation, employers and employees must wholeheartedly embrace lifelong learning. This will require some sacrifice from both, which is just another word that means "investment." Innovators and entrepreneurs need to be as concerned about talent development as they are about technology development. Unless both employers and employees are willing to invest energy and resources into lifelong learning and entrepreneurs connect with the talent development system, there can be no return on investment for companies or career-seekers. This means we need new kinds of investments across a wide range of human-capital requirements. This will produce a better alignment between the economic-development strategies of regions, which are being driven by the imperatives of globalization and rapid innovation. When investments in workforce development and education strategies are better aligned with business strategies, this will assure the near-term, intermediate, and long-term payoffs the country needs. Without this commitment to investing energy and resources into reskilling and lifelong learning, there will be little return on investment for existing and growing companies or career-seekers.

Let's put this in historical perspective. In the days before 911-emergency phone systems, the way to warn a community about impending danger was to literally sound an alarm, such as a fire call box or the village bell. The importance of heeding warnings when someone sounds the alarm is a recurring literary theme through the ages. Three episodes in the last decade of American history also clearly bear this out. Think of how events might have turned out differently if America had not ignored these alarms.

In the financial world, the immeasurable damage caused by Bernie Madoff and the largest con game in history could have been avoided. Madoff, who is currently serving a 150-year sentence in federal prison, was arrested in 2008 for orchestrating an $18 billion Ponzi scheme that swindled money from thousands of investors. According to the Securities and Exchange Commission, unlike the promoters of many Ponzi schemes, the phony account statements from Madoff showed moderate, but consistently positive returns—even during turbulent market conditions. But consider what the outcome would have been if the SEC watchdogs had listened to the financial advisor who risked his life and career for ten years by sending detailed memos to the SEC on how Madoff was running a fraud of the highest order. For instance, one of the many red flags was that the accounting firm supposedly auditing Madoff's company was a three-person team in a thirteen-by-eighteen-foot office in New York (hardly adequate space to monitor a multibillion-dollar firm). Because the SEC watchdogs did not heed the alarm, many unfortunate individuals had their lives ruined and charities were cheated out of billions of dollars.

Remember when Hurricane Katrina pounded the Gulf Coast in 2005? Prior to the hurricane making landfall, scientists and engineers warned of the deadly consequences if the levees failed during a storm surge. One university researcher was later compared to a disaster-movie character, the "workaholic scientist who understands the impending disaster that no one else really sees" and battles against "overwhelming odds, skeptical colleagues, and petty bureaucrats." But this scientist was not alone in sounding the alarm. For years, the Army Corps of Engineers warned what a powerful hurricane could do to New Orleans and the area's transportation, energy, and petrochemical facilities. The Army Corps of Engineers formally notified Washington that a hurricane could knock out two of the big pumping stations that must operate night and day just to keep the city dry, and also reported that several levees had settled and would soon need to be raised. Unfortunately, shoring up the Gulf Coast was not a priority, a decision that had deadly consequences.

Finally, the near collapse of the banking industry in 2007–2008 was not a disaster without warning. Washington was cautioned as long as a decade ago by bank regulators, consumer advocates, and a handful of lawmakers that subprime loans represented a mortgage-meltdown risk to the economy. Here are just a few examples. As far back as 2001, advocates for low-income homeowners had argued that mortgage providers were making loans to borrowers without regard to their ability to repay. The *Los Angeles Times* reported that long before the mortgage crisis began rocking Main Street and Wall Street, a top FBI official made a frightening prediction: The booming mortgage business, fueled by low interest rates and soaring home values, was starting to attract shady operators and billions in losses were possible. "It has the potential to be an epidemic," an FBI official in charge of criminal investigations told reporters in September 2004. "We think we can prevent a problem that could have as much impact as the S&L crisis," he added reassuringly. Ironically, his enforcement budget was cut. In 2005 regulators strongly warned banks that exotic mortgages were often inappropriate for buyers with bad credit. These were the same banks that soon collapsed or had to be bailed out. And if banks weren't listening, some investors were. Many foresaw the mortgage meltdown and made a fortune betting on it. Taxpayers are paying for this failure to heed alarms in two ways: an economic meltdown and a huge tax bill.

While these incidents are in the past, we can still learn a valuable lesson from them. This book is sounding a different kind of alarm. The authors are optimistic that the dream of good jobs for all can still be achieved. But only if America heeds the warning that we need to not only invest in innovation that leads to job creation, but we also must invest in necessary "reskilling" so that the United States is not forced to export jobs or import labor. Policymakers, entrepreneurs, and job-seekers all have a role to play. Our future prosperity and the hope of good jobs for all depend upon it.

For these reasons, the information in this book is divided into two sections and an addendum. Section One is a detailed analysis of America's job gap, the disparity between the good jobs being created by small-business innovation in the U.S. and the lack of American workers with the skills to fill these good jobs. The weight of the data clearly demonstrates something is terribly amiss with projections of economic recovery and the disproportionate job growth. Section Two of this book demonstrates that a region other than Silicon Valley can and should use innovation to create good jobs and community prosperity. As the section points out, this can only be accomplished through collaborative effort. There is much to be done by policymakers, entrepreneurs, and job-seekers if America is to close the job gap. For those who desire the numbers behind the analysis, the addendum provides a detailed look at America's unique culture of innovation, innovation ecosystems, and the forces that led to the growth of high-value jobs in the San Diego region. These deeper reflections on innovation and job creation are designed to help light the way as America redesigns its future.

Mary Walshok, Tapan Munroe & Henry DeVries

ACKNOWLEDGEMENTS

The authors of the book are thankful for the stimulating discussions and insights that many colleagues and collaborators have contributed to the creation of this book. We have been greatly benefited by our colleagues at the University of California.

Mary would like to thank Alla Reisner for her meticulous job in integrating the various pieces of the book, her careful reading of the three authors' contributions, and her help with the flow and structure of the final manuscript. With support from Michele Hegedus, she also typed the entire manuscript. We could not possibly have completed the manuscript on time without their helpful and consistently cheerful support. Mary would also like to acknowledge the ETA (Education and Training Administration) of the U.S. Department of Labor and, in particular, Eileen Pedersen, our program officer, for the opportunity to listen to America over a four-year period as the principal investigator for their evaluation of the first group of WIRED grants awarded to thirteen regional collaboratives across the United States focused on better aligning their innovation and talent-development systems. The experience awakened Mary to the absolute necessity of better aligning workforce-development strategies with innovation and entrepreneurship efforts as the path to renewing prosperity. It also made her painfully aware of how challenging it is to do so, given the attitudes, practices, and policies, which can be barriers to collaboration.

Tapan would like to thank his colleague Mark Westwind for valuable assistance researching occupational and employment trends.

Henry would like to thank his research team: Helen Chang, Jenny Lemmons, Marty Graham, Andrea Siedsma, Chris Stiehl, Donna Moore, Noonie Benford, and Lauren Bogart.

Finally, this book could never have come to pass without the commitment and drive of Arthur Chou and the team at WBusiness Books.

SECTION 1

A WORKFORCE
OUT OF ALIGNMENT

CHAPTER 1

Is the American Dream Dead?

R emember the good old days of booming business and plentiful jobs? In a period of high unemployment—hovering around 10 percent across the United States—the theme of this book may strike the reader as absurd. America's job crisis is not simply that there are too few good jobs to go around, but rather that there are not enough good workers for the multitude of jobs that U.S. companies need to fill today or that will soon become available.

The job losses precipitated by the poor strategic and managerial practices of major United States industries like automotive and finance, and their subsequent effects on sectors such as construction and retail, have been wrenching for America. While major, these job losses also mask deeper trends affecting the job challenges and opportunities ahead. As a nation, our global competitiveness is at risk if we do not understand and engage these keys to our long-term future. The opportunities for American employers to remain competitive and for employees to have rewarding careers will be diminished if we do not understand and engage the realities of America's workforce needs.

The headlines say it all. Thomas Friedman, writing in the *New York Times*, urges "Start-Ups, Not Bail-Outs," pointing to the mounting data that large, established industries are cutting jobs while small start-up and growth companies are creating jobs.[1] The National Academy of Sciences, the National Science Foundation, and the U.S. Council on Competitiveness have all published reports projecting significant disconnects between the supply of workers with technical, engineering, math, and science skills and the rapid growth of knowledge-based industries.[2] The American Society of Training and Development (ASTD) and organizations such as Manpower Temporary Services forecast significant skill gaps in the job market due to the mobility of workers, but, more important, due to the flood of retiring baby boomers.[3]

It was James Truslow Adams who first coined the term "the American Dream" in his 1931 book *The Epic of America*.[4] He writes that the American Dream is:

> *"... that dream of a land in which life should be better and richer and fuller for everyone, with opportunity for each according to ability or achievement."*

It is not only the dream of nice cars and high wages. More significant, it is a dream of a social order where any man or woman can attain a secure livelihood based on his or her innate abilities, not just the fortuitous circumstances of his or her birth or position.

The American Dream is core to America's national ethos. We all believe in democratic values, and equal opportunity represents the key to our personal and national economic prosperity. In everyday language it means prosperity and a good life for all Americans. This dream includes a good job, home ownership, and a bright future for one's children.

Fundamental to the realization of the American Dream is the opportunity to work and earn a fair return on one's labor. Without a job, none of the other critical needs such as home, education for children, a healthy and comfortable life, or a respectable existence, is possible.

The American Dream has been a magnet for millions of immigrants who come to this land, often under difficult circumstances, in search of a better life. The history of America is a one of people immigrating to this country and migrating across the country, looking for good jobs. Jobs are why millions of people from all parts of the world have come to this country for over three centuries. The belief that in America, that one can always find a good job and advance in his or her career has been a fundamental driver of our success for generations. It is buttressed by

> " The American Dream may still be viable, but job opportunities are being shaped by very different forces in the 21st century than they were in the 20th century."

the equally strong belief that in this country, anyone with a good idea and the "grit" can not only find a job, but create his own business. As Joel Kotkin's book "Tribes"[5] so dramatically underscores, the history of America is a history of successive waves of newcomers building small enterprises to eke out a living for their families: Irish pubs in Boston, Jewish tailors in New York, German shopkeepers in the Midwest, and Korean grocers in Los Angeles. And today, these hardworking immigrants from Central Europe, China, and India are starting global technology companies in Texas, New York, and California. This is and has been the American Dream. The critical question, at this moment in time, is whether or not that dream is dead. Is it still possible to get a good job or build a successful business in light of the recently battered economy?

THE JOBLESS RECOVERY

The American Dream may still be viable, but job opportunities are being shaped by very different forces in the 21st century than they were in the 20th century. The worst recession since the Great Depression of the 1930s has eliminated more than eight million jobs in the U.S. Almost every industry except health care has shed jobs during the major recession of 2008-2009. The impact has been most serious on residential construction, automobile manufacturing, retail, and banking. Meanwhile, the U.S. gross domestic product, the broadest measure of economic activity, continues to recover in 2010. Real GDP growth for the U.S. was positive for the first three quarters of 2010 (see Figure 1). However, the U.S. job machine appears to have stalled and unemployment remains in the 9 percent to 10 percent range (See Figure 2).

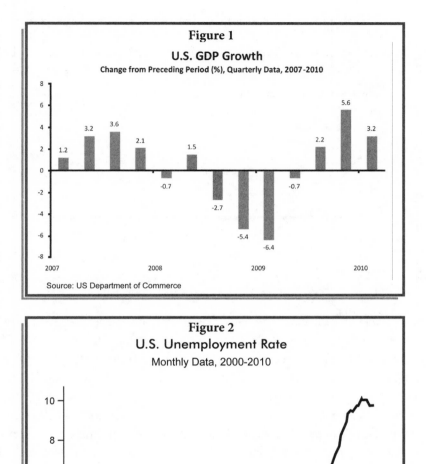

Figure 1

U.S. GDP Growth

Change from Preceding Period (%), Quarterly Data, 2007-2010

Source: US Department of Commerce

Figure 2

U.S. Unemployment Rate

Monthly Data, 2000-2010

Source: US Bureau of Labor Statistics

In most economic recoveries, jobs come back vigorously as soon as the recession is over. In the aftermath of the 2008–2009 recession (that started in December 2007), this has not happened. Job growth continues to languish despite three quarters of significant growth in GDP. Comparison with the recessions of 1957 and 1973 (Figure 3) clearly shows the slow job recovery time for the 2007 recession. It is actually the slowest since World War II.

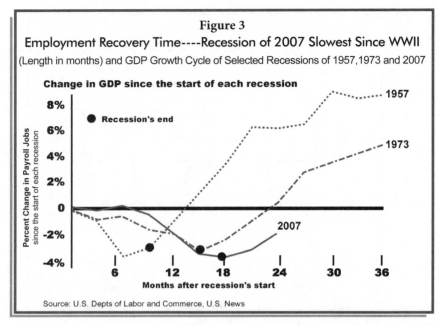

Figure 3

Employment Recovery Time----Recession of 2007 Slowest Since WWII

(Length in months) and GDP Growth Cycle of Selected Recessions of 1957,1973 and 2007

Change in GDP since the start of each recession

Source: U.S. Depts of Labor and Commerce, U.S. News

Why has this happened? There are two reasons for the anemic job growth in the current recovery. First, the recent recession hit the manufacturing and construction industries especially hard. Additionally, the consumer-based industries have seen precipitous declines and, while some of these jobs will likely return, others may not come back due to the high levels of personal debt which may curtail spending for a long period. As shown in Figure 4, the only sectors that have remained unscathed throughout the recent recession are health care and education.

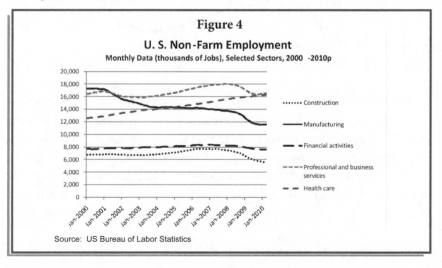

Figure 4

U. S. Non-Farm Employment

Monthly Data (thousands of Jobs), Selected Sectors, 2000 -2010p

Source: US Bureau of Labor Statistics

The second reason for the anemic job growth is structural changes in the United States economy resulting from the recession of 2008–2009 and the global financial-markets crisis. The impact of lower asset prices (e.g., home prices), tighter credit, and higher energy costs translates into a major structural shift in the U.S. economy—a shift from debt and domestic consumption to savings and exports.[6] This shift will result in a very different mixture of jobs, as well as the determination of where the centers of job growth will be.

Consumer spending has dominated the American economy for a long time. Since 1950 the share of consumer spending in the GDP has been in the 60–70-percent range. Prior to the recent financial crisis, it stood at nearly 70 percent. Easy credit made it possible for consumers to borrow and live beyond their incomes. The new era of tight credit (i.e., greater due diligence in lending) will mean that, although consumption will grow, it is unlikely to grow at rates faster than income. For the last two decades, America has been living beyond its means, ushering in an era of increasing spending deficit. Those days are over. Baby boomers can no longer depend on ever-increasing home prices as a base for their retirement. They have to begin saving more and spending less.

With rising consumer savings and shrinking domestic consumption and domestic spending, American businesses, out of necessity, are looking more and more to overseas markets. A boom in American exports to emerging markets will be in high-end manufacturing such as microprocessors, high-tech equipment, medical devices, pharmaceuticals, software, and high-end services such as engineering and oil processing, as well as creative endeavors such as film, architectural design, and advertising. The export boom will be led by American companies that already have considerable global presence. Examples of such firms include Intel and Microsoft. With advances in communication and digital technology, more and more American businesses will be able to export their products and services, as they can be sold relatively easily using new technology. This represents an enormous opportunity for entrepreneurs and start-ups.

In addition to tighter credit and lower consumer borrowing, the third trigger for the structural change in the U.S. economy has been higher energy prices. Throughout the 1990s a robust dollar and plenty of oil kept prices low for Americans. This situation changed a few years before the recent recession with a rise in demand for oil from emerging economies such as China and India, and a falling dollar. Oil prices have risen sharply since the early 1990s. More increases are undoubtedly coming.

The combination of higher oil prices, a growing national interest in energy conservation, and the lag in home sales is likely to result in a slowdown in suburban growth and increased interest in moving into areas near the urban core and edge cities closer to jobs and services. Population growth has, in fact, slowed in the suburbs and risen in the cities.[7]

An economy shifting away from domestic consumption to high-end exports is also likely to gravitate to metropolitan cores because such firms depend on attracting younger, more educated, and more creative workers who typically prefer living in vibrant city centers. Richard Florida, an urban-planning expert from the University of Toronto, suggests in a 2009 article in the *Atlantic* that the new economy does not just focus on making and moving goods from one place to another, but is increasingly involved in moving ideas from one place to another.[8] He concludes that the places that will prosper most in the new century are those that have the highest velocity of ideas and the highest density of talented and creative people. He is, of course, talking about vibrant cities such as San Francisco, Boston, and Austin that have been magnets for younger knowledge workers and intellectual talent. Our take on this issue is that as long as Americans want to own single-family homes and their love affair with the automobile continues, suburbia will remain a destination for younger families with children, and suburban living will remain a significant option for many Americans. Understandably, suburbs closer to vibrant cities will become increasingly attractive. Nonetheless, structural changes in the American economy portend major changes in the United States jobs picture, both in terms of different kinds of jobs and a different spatial distribution of jobs across the country.

That is why this book asserts that a critical approach to closing America's job gap is to address, head on, the challenges and opportunities arising from four forces, which go beyond the immediate recession and relate to longer-term structural shifts. These have been given far too little attention in the national conversation about global competitiveness and good jobs for all, and can be summed up in terms of attention to four forces, which could help close the job gap:

- The role innovation and entrepreneurship, primarily through small businesses, plays in job creation.

- The role recurrent and rapid changes in markets and technology (aka globalization) plays in the evolving knowledge and competencies required in all jobs

- The role demography plays in shaping where skills will be needed and who will be skill-ready for openings being created, including by retirements

- A growing skills gap, a significant component of which is based on the lack of early alignment between innovators, who create the value-added new businesses and job opportunities, and educators and workforce developers, who are lagging in their knowledge about what is shaping their regional economy.

Yes, Virginia, there is a job crisis in America. But it is not simply a crisis based on the current recession. It is a crisis based, in large part, on looking at work and jobs through the lens of an old industrial economy built upon large, vertically integrated companies and operating in an environment with minimal global competition (particularly in the United States in the 1950s and 1960s). It is built on a history of local communities relying on large or leading industry employers for good jobs and regional economic prosperity. It is built on a longing for stability over time, which is no longer possible in an era of rapid technological change and the globalization of the producers and consumers of goods and services.

Clearly, the recent precipitous decline in employment opportunities in traditional manufacturing and in construction is a very real and present challenge. While we recognize that these forces are all at work, the point of this book is to suggest to the reader that the heart of America's problems is the skills gap based on trends just noted. This skills gap has been accumulating over a number of decades, but is dramatically apparent today because of the following interrelated developments, which shape the needs and demands of America's workforce in dramatic ways:

- The speed with which new technologies and processes, as well as emerging markets, is expanding and shaping the demand for new products requiring new skills.

- This speed, in turn, gives rise to the rapid obsolescence of basic education and training and the need for continuous learning across the life cycle, as well as higher and higher levels of educational achievement among all categories of workers.

- The imminent retirement of close to 25 million baby boomers in a variety of occupations, which require skills for which we may not have a currently ready workers – skills ranging from plumbing, welding, and computer pro gramming to marketing, financial management and laboratory research management.

The bottom line is that the job crisis we face in America is not only about the immediate recession. It is also about the lack of alignment between the skills of the American workforce and the speed with which technology development and global trends are taking us. Here are two examples. One of the authors of this book contributed to a plan to assist a global-technology company, with facilities in San Diego, in coming up with a strategy to immediately find or train three hundred engineers. The strategic group met with the mayor of San Diego, who recognized the importance of retaining the San Diego division of this internationally known company, rather than letting it move to another state or country. The mayor understood that the three hundred engineering jobs required another three hundred non-engineering jobs in business and support services, in supplier relationships, as well as in clerical and custodial jobs. Later the same week, the coauthor was contacted by a large Missouri university that had moved one of its spinoff companies to San Diego, asking if the global-technology company could be helped in finding engineers. The company moved to San Diego to be in the innovation-rich ecosystem. But once the start-up was settled, the company had difficulty finding the kind of engineers it needed. The lack of alignment in innovation and workforce development is threatening the ability of U.S. companies to remain in many regions, as well as threatening the ability of innovative start-up companies to achieve necessary growth.

Outsourcing is as much a function of needing skills that can't be found in the United States as it is a result of the desire to find "cheap" labor. The skills gap is a function of failing to recognize skill needs and prepare needed workers for new and emerging technologies that are transforming the content of all work, as well as creating new industries and new job opportunities with appropriate education and training strategies.

In February of 2010, the Investigative Reporting Workshop at the American University School of Communication in Washington, D.C., reported that, of the more than $2 billion in federal stimulus money focused on supporting the growth of the renewable-energy industry and clean-energy jobs, close to 80 percent was flowing to foreign companies. For example, large grants, particularly in the wind-energy sector, intended to support the construction of turbines for new windmill farms across the United States, could not be spent in the U.S. because of the lack of American companies with a skilled workforce ready to manufacture and install this technology.[9]

This dilemma was reinforced by research visits made by one of the authors of this book to the state of Michigan over a three-year period during which the governor was leading an impressive effort to build wind-energy farms and require LEED-certified practices in the construction, maintenance, and repair of all publicly funded infrastructure, such as roads, bridges, and government buildings. During those visits it became clear—even though there had been government and private funds allocated for these sorts of clean energy initiatives—that there had been little or no analysis of what sorts of production capacities, supplier networks, and skilled workers would be needed to take advantage of these new opportunities. As a result, in the traditionally industrial state of Michigan— with an unemployment rate in some places as high as 20 percent—contracts for the windmill farms in north-central Michigan primarily went to non-Michigan companies, including some foreign manufacturers and suppliers from countries such as Denmark. Additionally, in the early stages, it was difficult to find qualified painters and construction workers to bid on new LEED-certified infrastructure projects. The most dramatic example of this was, initially, the absence of any Michigan bidders on an opportunity to repaint the Mackinac Bridge in compliance with LEED-certified standards. The contract represented a year's worth of work for six hundred painters, and yet no one in Michigan—where there was high unemployment in the construction and building-maintenance industries—was qualified to bid at that time. Fortunately, a nimble school, Mott Community College in Flint, Michigan, developed a fast-track training program.

This disconnect between both public and private investments in new and promising technologies and the tooling, manufacturing, production, and workforce capabilities in the United States is one of the sources of persistent unemployment rates. It was not the initial goal of Michigan Governor Jennifer Granholm to find companies outside the state. However, she had to do so because there was not a critical mass of superior technology and an already skilled workforce to take advantage of the opportunity. The governor of Michigan would have had to accept a bid from a California firm to paint the Mackinac Bridge had it not been for an enterprising community college stepping up to the plate and offering to train the painters within the timeframe and standards needed so that those jobs could go to Michigan citizens and not Californians.

A CASE IN POINT: THE PROMISE OF GREEN COLLAR JOBS

In 2007, Van Jones, a Yale Law School-educated community organizer from Oakland, California, wrote a book which, to his surprise, became an instant *New York Times* bestseller: *The Green Collar Economy: How One Solution Can Fix Our Two Biggest Problems*. The early pages of the book are especially relevant to the point we are trying to make about the skills gap, and especially about how the skills gap is occurring across a wide range of occupations, moving from skilled and semi-skilled to highly-skilled-professional and even Ph.D.-level jobs. But all of these will require reskilling, upskilling, and continuous education and training across the life span of workers. Jones asks the question:

> *"So who will do the hard and noble work of actually building the green economy? The answer: millions of ordinary people, many of whom do not have good jobs right now. According to the National Renewable Energy Lab, the major barriers to a more rapid adoption of renewable energy and energy efficiency are not financial, legal, technical, or ideological. One big problem is simply that green employers can't find enough trained, green-collar workers to do all the jobs."[10]*

The thrust of Jones's book is a call to action through a variety of policy initiatives that can support the growth of green-energy technologies and companies as well as the thousands of jobs that will be created by these companies. He describes how hundreds of thousands of green-collar jobs will likely be in weatherizing and energy-retrofitting every building in the United States. He comments that "the main piece of technology in the green economy is a caulking gun."[11]

He goes on to describe that another bit of green high technology is the clipboard, which is the tool used by energy auditors as they point out energy-saving opportunities to homeowners, renters, and landlords retro-fitting buildings.[12] His list of some of the key tools for achieving the promise of the green economy include not only finding new manufacturing technologies to convert such things as solar, wind, geothermal, and green algae into cost-effective forms of energy, but "wrapping hot-water heaters with blankets, blowing insulation, plugging holes, repairing cracks, hauling out old appliances, installing new boilers or furnaces, replacing old windows with the double- glazed kind." As he remarks, "We will also need well-trained, well-paid workers in a range of green industries: materials reuse and recycling, water management, local and organic food production, mass transportation, and more."[13]

Linking job development and job creation with the innovation process holds enormous promise in the emerging green economy because, as Jones points out, these are middle-skill jobs and/or new-skill jobs for which many Americans, through education and training, can be highly qualified. Again, quoting Jones:

> *"Like traditional blue-collar jobs, green-collar jobs range from low-skill, entry-level positions to high-skill, higher-paid jobs and include opportunities for advancement in both skills and wages. Think of them as the 2.0 version of old-fashioned blue-collar jobs, upgraded to respect of the Earth and meet the environmental challenges of today . . . Like blue-collar jobs, green-collar jobs can pay family wages and provide opportunities for advancement along a career track of increasing skills and pay . . . Much of the work we have to do to green our economy involves transforming the places we live and work in and changing the way we get around. These jobs are difficult or impossible to outsource."[14]*

We also know, given research in American research universities today and the phenomenal job growth in the green economy in places such as Denmark, Sweden, and Germany, that the green economy will require new workers with new skill sets, many of them in technical and engineering fields. Renewable-energy technicians; biofuels processing; computer control operators, who can cut steel for wind towers; and mechanics who can fix electric as well as internal-combustion engines are examples that Jones provides in his book. In addition, architects and engineers designing housing, shopping malls, hospitals, and business offices will require new skills and new kinds of professionals on their teams in order to design and execute according to new construction, transportation, heating, and cooling standards. All of these are promising job-creation activities. However, the potential of this diverse range of new jobs in the green economy depends on the willingness of local communities, states, and the federal government to recognize the inextricable link between creating innovative products and processes and equipping an American workforce with the skills to design and manufacture those new products, engage the new processes, and maintain sustainable practices across a variety of industries.

Innovation is, clearly, what is driving job growth in the United States; however, it is no longer the innovation that occurs within big companies that expands job opportunities. Rather, it is the innovation taking place within small entrepreneurial companies that create new opportunities. Innovation in a large-company context is typically driven by an interest in increasing competitiveness and profitability, usually through efficiencies that result in more output from fewer workers. In contrast, small entrepreneurial companies are introducing new products, seeking new markets, and even creating new markets. They are creating job opportunities as they grow and expand. A November 2009 Kauffman Foundation report, *Where Will the Jobs Come From?* suggests that as recently as 2007, two-thirds of net new jobs were created by start-up firms less than five years old.[15]

THE FUTURE IS NOT OVER

The United States has a long history of westward expansion, economic growth and increasing diversity because it is a nation of successive generations of immigrants. The image of America around the world as a land of opportunity has been based on this history of expanding opportunities and the potential for good jobs for all. The authors of this book do not believe that the future is over. However, the job-expansion opportunities and the arenas in which good jobs for all will be available are tied to very different conditions today than in the past. If we understand and embrace them, we can realize a bright future; if we ignore them, we are in danger of becoming a second- or third-tier economy. Closing America's job gap requires a focus on innovation, technology, and globalization in new and creative ways so that we can realize America's promise.

This phenomenon of workforce capacity lagging behind technological and regulatory shifts that supposedly hold great promise for economic re-generation recurs again and again. It occurs, in part, because there is not the same tradition in the United States of coupling workforce development with economic development that one finds in many other parts of the world. It is also the case that United States companies, compared to companies in countries such as Sweden and France, spend much less time on the educa-tion, training, and reskilling and up-skilling of their workers. In Sweden, for example, a typical worker spends as many as twenty days a year in educa-tion and training. In the United States, the typical worker spends a quarter or less of that amount of time in education and training.

Closing America's job gap can, first and foremost, be achieved through a better articulation of what skills are needed not only today, but are likely to be needed in three months, six months, or twelve months, based on rapid changes in technology and in regulatory requirements. This requires—not only at the federal level, but most particularly at the regional level—ongoing conversations between the drivers of regulatory change and technological innovation: employers in both existing industries and emerging employ-ment sectors, and the workforce-development education-and-training sys-tem, which includes federally funded programs, regional community col-leges, proprietary institutions, as well as universities.

In those communities that are able to support high levels of innova-tive companies, such as San Diego and Seattle, one finds very cutting-edge forms of education and training to keep up with the economic and technological developments in a way that serves the competitive needs of the regional economy, along with with assuring good jobs for residents in the region. Dynamic innovation regions, which have significant sector growth such as the computer industry in Austin, the software industry in Seattle, and the wireless and life-sciences industry in San Diego, are places where you will find equally innovative and varied approaches to education and training, resulting in a qualified workforce for fast-growing, globally competitive companies.

CHAPTER 2

America's Shifting Employment Profile

The whole nation is asking the question "Where are the jobs?" This is, of course, a pressing question for the eight-to-fifteen million unemployed and underemployed workers in the United States. Although many government officials declare that the recession has technically ended, to millions of Americans who are struggling to make ends meet the announcement seems irrelevant. As media pundits proclaim this to be a "jobless recovery" and look for scapegoats to blame, more rational voices acknowledge that this will be a long, slow recovery when it comes to jobs growth, but caution that the solutions to our predicament are complex. This is not simply a matter of spending our way back to the way things used to be. Things will not be the way they were in the past; in this chapter we want to help employers and employees understand why this is the case.

Before the question "Where are the jobs?" can be pondered, it's important to ask "Where *were* the jobs?" Certainly, the recession wiped out many good jobs in what most people thought were relatively "recession-proof" occupations (e.g., financial services). However, the recession only exacerbated trends that have been evolving for many years in other sectors (e.g., manufacturing). Recession or not, this country's employment profile is experiencing permanent change and the reality is that many of the jobs that have been lost are gone for good. This is particularly hard to hear if you're an older worker with a limited education and years of work experience in yesterday's occupations. There's hope, however, but it'll take hard work—and time.

So what did the country's employment profile look like twenty years ago, as the 1990s started and the nation's economy teetered on the brink of the 1990–91 recession? And what did it look like some eighteen years later as we entered what would be the worst recession in memory? Figure 5 tells a number of interesting stories.

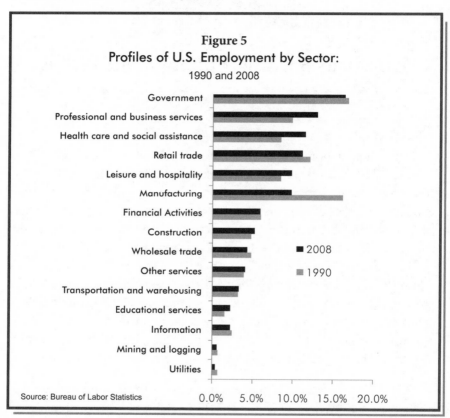

Figure 5
Profiles of U.S. Employment by Sector:
1990 and 2008

Source: Bureau of Labor Statistics

First of all, the most obvious change is the dramatic difference in manufacturing employment. This is a story that's been told and retold, with the causes being well known: outsourcing, automation, and increasing worker productivity as a result of technological advances. Of course, this story is not quite so simple as it also involves cheap foreign labor, the rise of China and India as manufacturing powerhouses, and the inability of some of our domestic manufacturing companies to maintain their global competitive positions (e.g., U.S. automakers) against aggressive foreign innovators. Fortunately, it seems that the Great Recession may be viewed in hindsight as the Great Wakeup Call, as the cheap dollar has rekindled hope and opportunity for those United States manufacturers that are competitive in the global marketplace.

The second impression that jumps out of Figure 5 is the significant gains in professional and business services, health care, and education. Again a cliché, America has experienced a shift to a service-based economy. Whether it's in helping businesses grow or helping people stay healthy, Americans are making fewer things with their hands and doing more with their heads. And, as several boom cycles have made more people wealthy and a lower dollar exchange rate has made travel to the United States more attractive, other service sectors like leisure and hospitality have also thrived.

Other stories also emerge. For example, despite the assertion many make about a growing government sector, its share of total employment actually declined slightly over the eighteen years (and several administrations) between 1990 and 2008. Certainly, the actual number of government workers has increased, but so has the size of the United States population and, with that, the need for government services, including roads, water systems, administration of justice, law enforcement, etc. Note also the slight decline in the information sector. This sector has experienced a wild ride over the last twenty years with a series of booms and busts including the dot-com boom/bust cycle in tandem with the rise and rapid fall of the telecom industry. Both off-shoring and automation (i.e., smarter hardware) have taken their tolls in the information sector.

IMPACT OF THE GREAT RECESSION

Recession or not, our country's employment profile has been changing and the shift has clearly been toward knowledge-based occupations such as those in business, health care, and education. That said, how has the Great Recession impacted employment? To find out, we looked at the number of jobs gained and lost in the nation's primary employment sectors between 2008 and 2010 (see Figure 6).

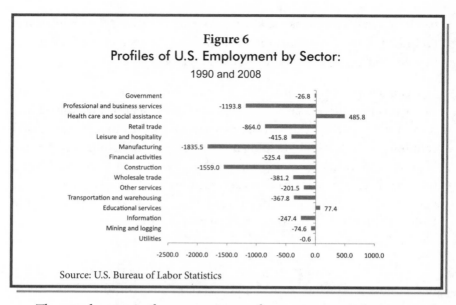

Figure 6
Profiles of U.S. Employment by Sector:
1990 and 2008

Source: U.S. Bureau of Labor Statistics

The good news is that two sectors of our economy, education and health care, actually grew during the recent recession, driven primarily by steady changes in demographics. Boomers are getting older and their kids are having kids. The rest of the jobs picture is a portrait of pain: significant job losses in every other sector. Certainly this has been a major recession, but how severe? Understanding the severity of these job losses will give us an important insight into the pathway to reemploying our idle workforce.

To get a perspective on how to assess the impact of the recession, we looked at the number of jobs lost in the nation's primary employment sectors between 2008 and 2010 and compared these losses to changes in those sectors during the period 1990 to 2008. What we found is sobering (see Figure 7).

The bad news is that, in the recent two-year period between January 2008 and March 2010, some sectors lost 30 percent to 80 percent of the job gains that had been accrued over the previous eighteen years. Employment in information and construction sectors is back to the levels they were in the early '90s. Over half of the job gains in the wholesale-trade sector that took almost two decades to create vaporized in two years. And, in the manufacturing sector, job losses between 2008 and 2010 equaled over 40 percent of the total losses in that sector over the previous eighteen years—a massive punch in the gut of America's industrial heartland.

Figure 7
Comparison of Job Gains/Losses:
1990 to 2008 and 2008 to 2010

Industry Sector (Jobs in Thousands)	Net Job Gains/Losses 1990-2008	Net Job Gains/Losses 2008-2010 (#)	Recession Change (Jobs in Thousands)
Information	295.7	-247.4	-83.7%
Transportation and warehousing	1,030.5	-367.8	-35.7%
Other services	1,253.5	-201.5	-16.1%
Wholesale trade	674.4	-381.2	-56.5%
Construction	1,894.8	-1,559.0	-82.3%
Financial activities	1,529.6	-525.4	-34.4%
Manufacturing	-4,293.9	-1,835.5	42.8%
Leisure and hospitality	4,149.7	-415.8	-10.0%
Retail trade	2,101.0	-864.0	-41.1%
Professional and business services	6,885.6	-1,193.8	-17.3%

The conclusion one can draw from Figure 7 is that it's probably unrealistic to expect all or even most of the approximately eight million jobs lost during the recent recession to come back quickly. And when new jobs are created, they may not come back in the same sectors or the same geographical places and, most certainly, not in the same skill areas. This is the changing nature of work.

WORK, JOBS AND WORKFORCE GROWTH

Work precedes employment. Better said, a more complete lineage for the venerable job is: Invention precedes innovation; innovation creates product and market opportunities that create work; work becomes jobs; and jobs become employment. We don't just hand out jobs for employment's sake; we employ people to do work that needs to be done (or at least that's the way it's supposed to be). So the real questions to be asked are: What needs to be done now and what will need to be done in the future? These questions and their answers are fundamental to how we approach our current and future job prospects. We are not going to recreate a bygone era of low-skill industrial jobs in an age of robotics. We are not going back to doing things by hand when machines are better, faster, and much cheaper. We are not going back to lifelong employment in one job that doesn't change for thirty years. Certainly, there will be many low-skill jobs that need to be done, but their value will also remain low as reflected by the wages paid for those positions.

Our nation's population is expected to increase by roughly 10 percent between 2008 and 2018, according to projections by the U.S. Census Bureau. Within the total population is our workforce—a cornerstone of our economy. The U.S. Bureau of Labor Statistics (BLS) expects the nation's workforce will grow by approximately 8 percent over the same period of time. The BLS notes that between 2008 and 2018, both the population and the workforce are expected to grow less than during the previous decade. This is partly due to the prediction that baby boomers (those born between 1946 and 1964) are expected to remain in the workforce longer than previous generations.[16]

Based on these two growth factors (population and workforce), our economy needs to create 150,000 to 200,000 new jobs every month of every year just to keep pace with the growth of our workforce, and in order to provide jobs for young people looking for their first jobs, people reentering the job market, and new jobs needed for legal immigrants. While we celebrate reports on the news of monthly jobs gains of 20,000 or 70,000 or even 100,000 new jobs in a month, we must remind ourselves that this is not enough—by a long shot.

The BLS makes a variety of long-term projections for job growth. These projections are useful as road maps to see where our economy is heading. To see where this map leads, we looked at the BLS *Occupational*

Outlook Quarterly for winter 2009–10 that documents the Bureau's job-growth projections in primary sectors from 2008 to 2018. Within these projections, we selected those occupations where job growth is expected to exceed 100,000. In effect, these occupations should hold the greatest hope for employing or reemploying our workforce (see Figure 8).

Figure 8
Top Areas of Job Growth:
2008-2018

Areas of Work	New Jobs:	
	2008-2018	Percent Growth
Taking Care of People	2,629,300	24.6 percent
Making Computers Work	677,700	23.7 percent
Taking Care of Business	655,100	22.7 percent
Building and Maintaining Our Infrastructure	1,488,200	12.9 percent
Teaching Children	860,400	12.7 percent
Designing Things; Solving Problems	178,300	11.0 percent
Keeping Businesses Running	1,909,800	12.0 percent
Selling Goods and Providing Basic Services	1,873,900	6.7 percent
Total New Jobs	10,272,700	

Source: U.S. Bureau of Labor Statistics

So, based on what we know today, where are the jobs of the future? The largest opportunities for job growth will be in the fields of Taking Care of People (health care)—understandable, as our country's population ages; Making Computers Work—clearly, our economy will need more programmers, network analysts, and systems managers; and Taking Care of Business in specialized areas such as accounting and human resources. America will also need more people Teaching Our Children and Rebuilding and Maintaining Our Infrastructure. And, while we also see large numbers of new jobs in Selling Goods and Providing Basic Services, the rate of growth in these occupations does not keep pace with the growth of the labor force.

Looking more deeply into the long-term jobs forecasts, we find that 30 percent of the thirty top job-growth occupations require a bachelor's degree or better. These jobs include doctors, nurses, teachers, and management analysts. The remaining 70 percent of the occupations require varying levels of work experience in the field (e.g., construction workers, medical assistants, executive assistants). Of course, there is a correlation between the level of education required for an occupation and the level of compensation. A summary of the top fifty best careers by *U.S. News* and *World Report* in May 2010 shows that only seven require less than an associate's degree and thirty-four require a bachelor's degree or higher.

What the Bureau of Labor Statistics cannot forecast easily are the hundreds of thousands of jobs likely to be created by innovative breakthroughs, new products, and new industries. Just as the World Wide Web and wireless-technology applications have given rise to thousands of new products, companies, and jobs unanticipated two decades ago, today's R&D in molecular biology, renewables, and agriculture biotechnology are likely to give rise to hundreds of thousands of new jobs or new skill requirements not in today's BLS forecasts.

THE CHANGING NATURE OF WORK

Bringing this all together, we find that long-term structural changes in the nation's economy are changing the job market. Factors such as automation, off-shoring, and technology-related increases in productivity are decreasing the need for low-skilled workers. The 2007–2009 recession has exacerbated the situation in some sectors, particularly manufacturing and construction. The recent recession wiped out decades of job growth and it will take years to return to the same employment levels. Nonetheless, there is hope that innovations in health-care technologies, clean tech, and renewables will create many good jobs that can replace many of the traditional manufacturing and skilled-trade positions lost in recent decades.

In a recently released study on America's job picture over the next decade, the Georgetown University Center on Education and the Workforce estimated that by 2018:

We will need twenty-two million new college degrees—but will fall short of that number by at least three million postsecondary degrees, associate's or better. In addition, we will need at least 4.7 million new workers with postsecondary certificates. At a time when every job is precious, this shortfall will mean lost economic opportunity for millions of American workers.[17]

In other words, we have a number of near-term challenges because of the need to immediately support emerging business and technology innovation. And that means focusing on adults. We have to update the skills of technical and service workers, manufacturing workers, engineers, managers, and health workers. We have a wonderful system of higher education that will allow us to do that, but it will require earlier and more frequent interaction between employers, educators, and the workforce-development system. America's trade unions, community colleges, regional workforce agencies, as well as four-year-degree- and Ph.D.-granting institutions, can be vital resources in closing the knowledge and skills gap we have today. We need to do an analysis of what skills are needed in the near term, i.e., six-to-twelve-month period, and that can only be done with employer-driven workforce-development strategies that provide fast-track certificates. There also is a number of significant mid-term (by that, we mean one to three years) skills that are needed in fields where highly skilled adults across the work spectrum need to be retrained and cross-trained to contribute to the sustainability of regional companies, as well as to contribute to the competitiveness of high-growth companies. In this sector, what is needed are provisions for already-employed workers. This includes training, retraining, cross-training, and professionalizing the American adult worker in the new knowledge and competencies we need for companies in a region to remain competitive.

Here, again, community colleges, state universities, management, and continuing education can address important needs. For the long term, we have the pipeline problem, and that's where K–12 activities, a wider range of technical-education programs within the community colleges, as well as interdisciplinary undergraduate and graduate degrees make a significant difference. The challenge within the K–16, post-graduate education, and the employer-driven continuing education system is that they rarely talk with one another, much less talk regularly with industry. If we are going to achieve alignment, we have to do a better job of developing a framework of lifelong learning that focuses on what needs to happen in foundational education relevant to the future. We must determine what can be done to reskill and expand competencies of the existing workforce so that—on short notice—communities and employers are ready to seize opportunities that contribute to company success, good jobs, and, ultimately, America's competitiveness.

> **"To fully understand the problem of this skills gap in America, we need to understand the changes in the nature of work over the last several decades."**

THE REAL JOB CRISIS

> *"Globalization and the emergence of other competitive nations have dramatically raised the bar for performance, creating pressure on those regions, industries, companies, and workers who are not prepared to meet the new standards of productivity. Simply being an American does not guarantee a high wage job anymore."*
>
> *- Professor Michael Porter, Harvard Business School*

There is a job crisis in America. Most people think it is about the absence of jobs as a result of the precipitous decline in employment opportunities resulting from the 2008–2009 recession. Analysts blame the recession; pundits blame the expanding use of outsourcing as a cost-cutting strategy in a growing number of business sectors; business leaders blame increasing competition from around the world, especially China. However, the real job crisis is about a long-festering skills gap and a broken education-to-employment system, which is dangerously disconnected from America's globally respected research leaders.

The skills of the American workforce are not aligned with where technology and global trends are heading, and the situation is getting worse. Outsourcing jobs is as much a function of needing skilled workers that you can't find in the United States as it is about cheaper labor. There is also a growing cultural problem with regard to the attitude of American workers who have assumed for decades that a good job is in some way an "entitlement." While this may have appeared to be true during the '50s and into the '60s, given the realities of a globally competitive jobs market, this is clearly no longer a reality.

THE SKILLS GAP & KNOWLEDGE WORKERS[18]

For the past decade or so, businesses and employers in the United States have been facing a critical challenge in finding the right people with the right skills to fill jobs in order to retain their competitive positions in the global economy. According to a 2009 study by the American Society for Training and Development,[19] the longstanding causes of the widening skills gap in the U.S. have been the rapid pace of the changing demands of today's workplace and the gap between educational attainment and the necessary skills for today's jobs. The prime causes of the skills gap are that jobs are changing and educational and training attainments are lagging behind the needs of the workplace.

To fully understand the problem of this skills gap in America we need to understand the changes in the nature of work over the last several decades. One of the major changes in the world of work has been the rise of knowledge workers. They are the people who think for a living or who are problem-solvers applying increasingly advanced technologies. Over the past decade, jobs involving transactions such as exchanging information and exchanging products and services have become the mainstay of the industrial economies of the world. Author Tom Davenport defines knowledge workers as workers who have high levels of expertise and education and the major purpose of their work involves the creation, distribution, and application of knowledge.[20]

Today in the United States, nearly 85 percent of work involves transactions, and the remaining 15 percent involves making things.[21] Davenport and others estimate that knowledge workers in the United States comprise about 28 percent of workers in the United States. Other estimates run as high as 45 percent. Regardless of which estimate is correct, one thing is certain: Knowledge workers are a very important part of our financial system, as they add great value to the economy. Businesses with a high percentage of knowledge workers form the fastest-growing sectors of our economy and that trend will accelerate in the twenty-first century. However, the increasing knowledge content of work is not only in an office or laboratory. In this age of computers and advanced technologies, construction, manufacturing, and the organization and delivery of retail services are equally affected. All jobs require literacy and the ability to understand complex processes and utilize sophisticated tools and methods.

THE EXTENT OF THE SKILLS GAP[22]

A 2009 nationwide assessment of the skills gap made by the 2009 ASTD study found that 79 percent of the 1,179 organizations polled reported that they were experiencing a skills gap. Nearly half of these organizations said that the skills of the current workforce were inadequate. Nearly a quarter of the respondents ranked the lack of qualified candidates as a primary reason for not hiring. Key findings of the 2008–2009 U.S. Bureau of Labor Statistics publication, the Occupational Outlook Handbook, involving job- and skills-related forecasts for the period 2006–2016 are:

- The growth sectors of our economy will be: education, health services, professional and business services, leisure and hospitality, wholesale and retail trade, transportation and utilities, finance, government, and information technology and services.

- Education and health-related services will add more jobs than any other industry sectors. Scientific and technical consulting, as well as management positions, will grow by nearly 78 percent. Demand for these services will be triggered by greater use of new technologies and greater complexity and sophistication of business.

- Demand for computer- and mathematics-related professionals, health-care practitioners, educators and trainers, and library-related professionals will be high.

- In 1991, less than half of United States jobs required skilled workers. By 2015, more than 75 percent of the jobs will require workers with special skills in science, technology, engineering, and mathematics (STEM). In other words, the STEM gap will increase significantly in the future.

Historically, America's economic success has been due to high achievements at all levels including higher education. According to a recent white paper by the National Center for Education and the Economy, as much as one-fifth of the growth in labor productivity was related to educational attainment and new technology in the workplace. It will be difficult to maintain the rising trend in worker productivity in light of the STEM gap and the general decline in investment in education at all levels from K–12 to college and graduate education. It is also imperative that community colleges, universities, and workforce-development entities do a better job of reskilling and up-skilling the adult workforce, so that they have the capacity to adapt to new technologies and integrate new competencies into their existing knowledge, skills, and experience.

The skills gap has been a serious structural problem in the U.S. economy for a while and will remain so, unless we fully acknowledge and understand the problem and do something substantial and lasting about it. If we fail, the skills gap will worsen and our competitiveness in the coming years will be further eroded. One of the challenges of the current economic recovery characterized by meager job growth and high unemployment is that businesses and other organizations are disinclined to hire from the ranks of the unemployed to close the skills gap in their organizations, even when they have vacancies. Instead, businesses create jobs requiring greater education and expertise, anticipating higher skill requirements down the road when the economy has recovered fully.[23] This means workers have to do a better job of anticipating and acquiring the new skills that will make them employable.

THE WIDENING GAP & IMPLICATIONS FOR COMPETITIVENESS[24]

America's skills-gap problem has been with us for a while and the implications are serious. In the twenty-first-century economy, it can seriously undermine our capacity to innovate, thereby slowing job growth, hindering productivity, and undermining national prosperity. A 1998 report entitled "Winning the Skills Race," by Amy Kaslow of the Council on Competitiveness, pointed out that prosperity in today's knowledge-intensive global economy depends on sustaining and enhancing the skills and education of our workforce. She concluded that our greatest competitive threat today is the widening skills gap of our workforce. Six years later, a 2005 survey by the National Association of Manufacturers (NAM) concluded that nearly 90 percent of manufacturing business owners and managers said that they had a moderate-to-severe shortage of skilled workers for positions such as machinist and technician. Nearly two-thirds reported a shortage of scientists and engineers; nearly half reported a lack of problem-solving skills among existing employees. More shocking was the fact that nearly 30 percent reported a lack of basic skills such as reading, writing, and basic-communication abilities among their employees. Many of these are jobs for which already skilled and educated adults can be reskilled through further education and training. The challenge is quite serious for businesses that rely heavily on science-and-technology-savvy workers. A National Science Foundation report published in 2005 estimated that job categories requiring a background in science and engineering would grow at nearly 5 percent a year. The report further stated that recent growth in this country's science and engineering workforce has been possible only due to the immigration of foreign-born scientists and engineers into the U.S.

The concern of the authors is that, with the rise in global demand for scientists and engineers, it will be difficult for the United States and other high-tech, knowledge-based economies to fill the rising demand for these high-skill workers. The problem is compounded further as many current scientific and engineering skills will become obsolete in a matter of a few years unless businesses, employees, and universities remain vigilant and proactive, and respond to the needs of maintaining and upgrading workforce skills in advanced fields. The challenge is equally significant for community colleges. They need to expand their technical-education programs to assure the skilled workforce needed in the new economy is available.

Business leaders are keenly aware of our global competitive challenge. They are fully aware of the fundamental connection between business performance and worker skills, and the crucial need to maintain a global perspective in leading their businesses. In a recent conversation, Marty Beard, president of Sybase 365—a subsidiary of California-based Sybase Inc., said:

> We all know that to compete globally, the United States needs strong and diverse talent driving our economy. In many ways, global economic competition is all about who can innovate the best and the fastest. The U.S. historically drove that innovation with a commitment to higher education, openness to immigration and diverse cultures, and a well-groomed investment and venture capital community. But all of this feels a bit 'frayed' recently, a bit worn-down. Many of us in the technology community, particularly in the software and wireless industries, travel extensively throughout the world. And we see the massive energy and innovation and drive in Asian economies like China and Singapore, and in emerging markets throughout Southeast Asia, the Middle East, even Africa, in places like Kenya. I was struck by the energy and optimism I witnessed during a recent trip to Beijing—it reminded me of the excitement and energy we all experienced in Silicon Valley and San Francisco during the emergence of the Internet.[25]

In answer to the question, "What should we do about our challenge?" Beard answered:

> Clearly, it is not too late, but we must re-energize America's commitment to education, to building the skills and driving the 'innovation culture' to stay ahead. We must work together to interconnect education, government, and corporate commitment to regional innovation. The power in the United States has always been about bringing these elements together. We need to get moving.[26]

The authors heartily agree.

THE SHRINKING TALENT POOL: A GLOBAL PHENOMENON[27]

Manpower Inc.'s 2009 worldwide talent survey involving thirt-nine thousand employers in thirty-nine countries concluded that nearly one-third of the employers were experiencing difficulty in filling the vacant jobs. This comes out to about two million unfilled jobs in the United

States and nearly 2.3 million vacancies in the European Union. This is amazing in a period where high unemployment and a purported lack of jobs has been the primary social and economic concern.

This trend is further verified by major staffing firms such as Robert Half International and Career Builders in their September 2009 report entitled "Employment Dynamics and Growth Expectations." A major conclusion of the report is that human-resources managers consider nearly 47 percent of their applicants to be unqualified. The problem is particularly serious in STEM (science, technology, engineering, and mathematics) related jobs. The skills and talent gap will become more acute as the economies around the industrial world pick up steam, and competition for hiring and retaining talented and skilled workers becomes intense.

What are the factors underlying this daunting situation? In a recent book entitled *Winning the Global Talent Showdown*, author Edward Gordon suggests that there are four major forces that are driving the global talent shortage. They are: 1) changes in workforce demographics, 2) globalization, 3) technology, and 4) the education-to-employment system.[28]

1. **Workforce Demographics:** According to the Social Security Administration, approximately seventy-eight million baby boomers will be retiring in the next twenty years, which works out to ten thousand a day for the next two decades. This will mean a huge loss of skill and expertise from the economy, particularly, since they will be replaced by only forty million Generation Xers in the next two decades. This translates into a huge net deficit in the already-shrinking talent pool. The problem is further exacerbated by the fact that with United States birthrates stable at the replacement rate, there will also be considerable shrinkage in the worker pool of ages 25 to 46. What is particularly alarming is that only one-fourth of United States organizations have given some thought to this impending crisis.

2. **Globalization:** For many people globalization is about off-shoring low-skill jobs to lower-wage countries. To others it is about importing to the United States high-skill international workers through H1-B visas. To many it implies United States companies

investing in overseas high-tech and high-skill factories. Globalization is all of these and more. The most striking thing about globalization is the emergence of China and India as high-tech and high-growth industrial giants. These two countries are progressing very rapidly in most high-tech fields. Although the United States has outsourced nearly six million low-skill jobs overseas in the period from 2000 to 2009, it is no longer a one-way flow of workers. China has eliminated nearly twenty million low-skill jobs as it continues to move up to higher-value manufacturing. Well-educated and skilled foreign-born workers who are presently employed in the United States are returning to their home countries because of higher wages and good opportunities there. Nearly 200,000 skilled and well-trained Chinese workers have returned to their homeland. In the last ten years nearly thirty thousand to forty thousand high-tech workers have returned to Bangalore, India, from the United States. This is reverse brain drain. For the last two decades, H1-B visas for foreign high-tech high-skill workers have made-up for the talent and skills shortage in the U.S. The billion-dollar question is how the U.S. will bridge the skills gap now that China and India have become major competitors for high-skill workers. Another complicating factor for the three top high-tech economies of the world—Japan, Germany, and the United States—is a severe drop in interest in STEM (science, technology, engineering, mathematics) subjects among students. In 2008, the first year of the recent recession, there were seventy-five thousand vacancies in STEM-related positions in Germany. Disinterest in STEM subjects will further exacerbate the skills and talent gap in the world.

3. **Technology:** When computers were introduced into the workplace in the 1950s and the 1960s, there was concern that the computer revolution would result in rising productive capacity and that would result in mass elimination of jobs. That has not happened. The IT revolution has actually created thousands of new products and services. However, what has happened is that a number of mid-level jobs such as filing, bookkeeping, and order-taking have been considerably re-

duced in the last several decades. Simultaneously, the number of knowledge-worker jobs involving thinking, analysis, and a high level of expertise in technology has risen a great deal. Quite simply, we have had a workplace revolution in the United States and the rest of the industrial world, including China and India in the last few decades.[29] Technologies will continue to be digitized and work can be moved anywhere in the world. The implications of this trend are quite serious for all countries. The United States will have to depend on the skills and talent of our own citizens to be able to compete globally. Simply put, innovation and economic development cannot be sustained without a continuously improving skill level of the workforce. This means an increased investment in continuous learning, reskilling, and up-skilling the American workforce.

4. **Education-to-Employment System:** One of the inescapable facts of the twenty-first century is that technology will not slow down. Technology will continue to accelerate and become more complex in most fields, including information technology, robotics, nanotechnology, biotechnology, plastic microchips, clean tech, and so on. This would require more skills, more education, and more talent in the workplace. The problem is that we already have a serious global shortage of skilled and talented workers. The shortage is particularly severe in fields related to STEM. Today, the most difficult-to-fill jobs around the world are for engineers, technicians, machinists, mechanics, and IT specialists.[30] But America has people with related skills who can, through education, become qualified for new skills and new jobs, which are constantly emerging. However, as noted above, this requires both a much bigger investment in continuous learning and, as important, much better alignment between the innovative sectors of our economy and the education-and-training segment of our economy.

The skills gap is a fundamental deficiency in our education-to-employment system. America must rethink its talent-creation system so that it is in tune with the realities of the fast-moving twenty-first-century cyber-economy.

INNOVATION, DIFFICULT ECONOMIC TIMES GO HAND IN HAND[31]

Many analysts expect difficult times ahead for innovation as the jobless economic recovery continues to create uncertainties about the robustness of the recovery. Many firms are still hesitant about spending money on innovation in uncertain times, thinking that such spending is peripheral to their main business. Some business leaders also think that spending on innovation is a distraction or just a frill.

This is a serious dilemma for the economy since innovation drives productivity and creativity, and they, in turn, drive prosperity. Innovation has never been as important as right now. It is not a luxury or a frill, it is an absolute necessity. America needs continued formation of new companies with innovative ideas for product creation. After all, some of these may become the HPs, the Googles, and Ciscos of tomorrow. Furthermore, we desperately need continued innovation in our existing businesses if we are to survive as the number-one economy in the world. Government spending alone will not solve our economic problem over the long haul.

There is good news: History is on America's side. There is a good chance that America's entrepreneurial culture will not let the U.S. down. Historically, that has been our major asset. There are two important issues to consider:

First, in the American economy, difficult economic times have not been deterrents for start-up businesses. They are the fundamental strategy for reviving our job-growth engine as they have been the prime source of job growth in our economy. Between 1985 and 2000 there would not have been a net increase in jobs in the U.S., had it not been for start-up businesses.

A large number of our stellar companies have been recession-era start-ups. They include companies known for their commitment to innovation, such as: IBM, Walt Disney, General Electric, HP, Kraft, Microsoft Corp., McDonalds, Hyatt Corp., Burger King Corp., FedEx Corp., CNN, MTV Networks, Trader Joe's, *Sports Illustrated*, and Electronic Arts.[32]

Why did these companies succeed? The founders discovered a market need and responded promptly to it in innovative and smart ways. The response worked even in difficult economic times. It should not be a surprise if the United States once again sees an increase in business start-ups even in the difficult conditions of the recession. Many of these are likely to be successful businesses in the next several years. Creation of new businesses is what entrepreneurial America does best. We can be optimistic that, once again, history will repeat itself. If the absolute number of start-ups increases, that should bring about increasing job opportunities. According to the Census Bureau, nearly all net job creation in the U.S. since 1980 occurred in start-up companies less than five years old. As the authors of the previously cited Kauffman Foundation report, *Where Will the Jobs Come From?* stated in a *Wall Street Journal* opinion piece, "Put more starkly, without new businesses, job creation in the American economy would have been negative for many years."[33]

Second, difficult economic times in the United States have been the mother of innovation.

Scott Anthony, in an article published in *Forbes* magazine[34], makes a convincing case that adversity encourages greater levels of innovation. What he suggests is that difficult economic times forces businesses to focus on developing smart and creative ways of delivering value and service to customers. They do not have the luxury of an economy flush with cash.

In hard times, companies are forced to reevaluate how they spend money. They have to cut expenses and still provide the quality of product and the same level of services. This challenge is the trigger mechanism that forces them to look for smarter and more effective ways of doing things. Perhaps one of the most dramatic examples of innovation triggered by difficult times is the case of Google during the dot.com recession of 2001. Struggling businesses had to save money on their advertising in the recession crunch. They discovered that advertising on search engines was easy, economical, and effective. As a result, 2001 was the breakthrough year for Google. The rest is history.

Rudy Provoost, the CEO of Phillips Lighting, summarized a very important point relating to what we are talking about: "In times of recession, the last thing you want to do is to cut off the oxygen. In times of recession, you need to work harder, run faster, so you need a lot of oxygen—and for me innovation is oxygen."[35]

Today Phillips Lighting is one of the world leaders in the development of fluorescent lighting. Its compact fluorescent bulbs use 70 percent less electricity than standard incandescent bulbs and last ten to fifteen times longer. Their street lighting system is reducing city energy bills by 50 percent or more. The company's policy during recessions is to manage innovation effectively by not reducing innovation activities. It is entirely possible that Phillips Lighting may gain market share from this recession.

During recessions, smart business leaders manage innovation effectively and do not cut back on it. After all, innovation is the lifeblood of a business. Let's not forget that a significant number of transformational innovations, such as the personal computer and the iPod, were introduced in difficult economic times. These recent start-ups today represent thousands of jobs.

While big companies, which are driven by increased competitiveness and profitability through efficiencies and streamlining, do not create lots of jobs, small companies will do so by introducing new products or seeking new markets. What all of this means is that we need approaches to innovation and entrepreneurship that also support job readiness. We need people to be ready for the jobs that are being created by small companies, as well as the positions opening up because of retirees or the introduction of new practices in large and existing companies.

WHERE ARE THE GOOD JOBS?

Chapter 4 of this book goes into a detailed discussion of a) where innovations are happening, b) the good jobs that will be needed by these sectors, and c) how individuals can be ready for these promising opportunities. In brief, the sectors include health information and related technologies because so much R&D and venture investment as well as new regulatory requirements are focused on creating integrated, readily accessible health records and procedures to provide better quality and more affordable health-care services. Similarly, such things as the focus on eradicating disease in third-world countries, extending health-care services and products in expanding economies like India and China, and meeting new demands for products and drugs among the world's aging population give rise to new companies and new jobs. There is an explosion of opportunities in clinical research; drug development; prosthetic devices and implants; cosmetics; and home-

and industrial-hygiene products. These trends drive R&D companies, as well as new product-manufacturing and distribution opportunities.

In a world where computer technology and the Internet have enabled the development of enormous amounts of data on an infinite array of topics, it is now possible to access and organize information in ways never before conceivable. Data mining has become a high-growth career opportunity as retailers attempt to understand consumers and manage inventory more effectively; municipalities manage transportation, police, fire, and utility services; charities track donors; social services evaluate intervention outcomes; and leisure and entertainment activities are Web supported. Career prospects are rich for people with data-mining skills in fields such as advertising, fraud detection, risk management, business intelligence, scientific research, program evaluation, law enforcement, health and social services, computer science, and statistics.

The future is bright if we can figure out how to better align education and training with America's areas of successful innovation. And the array of job growth opportunities is dazzling.[36] They include:

- **Repurposing America's skilled and technical workers for "new economy" applications, e.g., welders, pipe fitters, and mechanics.** Consider the fact that nearly 100 percent of welding-school graduates are finding rapid job placement. While about 500,000 welders are currently working in the U.S, the average welder is now nearing retirement age, with twice as many welders retiring as are being trained. As of 2010, it is estimated that the U.S. will be short more than 200,000 welders.

- **Home based businesses.** According to a *Bloomberg Business-Week* report from 2010, the number of self-employed who work exclusively from home increased from 3.47 million in 1999 to 4.34 million in 2005 (the latest figures available from the U.S. Census bureau). The total population of working from home at least some of the time increased from 9.48 million to 11.33 million in the same period. The report pointed out that the home-based workforce is well-educated and earns significant income.

In 2005, 46.5 percent had at least a bachelor's degree (compared to 27.2 percent of the total population over 25) and had a median family income of $63,648 (compared to the national median of $46,242 that year). These jobs include Web design and e-marketing, small-business skills, and accounting for such things as greeting cards, personal services, digital-media arts, and feature writing for the Web. Technology has transformed journalism and marketing, creating new ways for how information is conveyed. The new medium allows for more interactivity, as readers respond via comments or blogs.

- **Embedded engineering.** There are career options for software developers willing to learn some new tricks. Devices from phones, appliances, and televisions to automobiles and iPods, all use processors to run. These complex digital processors, or computers, are embedded systems, often built around a microprocessor core, that are designed by software engineers. According to the U.S. Bureau of Labor Statistics, software-engineering jobs are expected to increase by 32 percent in the next decade—one of the highest rates of all occupations.

- **Setting up an independent consulting practice.** Often there is work to be done, but no jobs. The trick is to offer to provide the labor as a true independent contractor. This is done to market your skills and experience whether in cabinet-making, catering, technical writing and editing, contract engineering, or strategic planning and team building. According to the U.S. Bureau of Labor Statistics, all areas of consulting should experience strong growth. For example, the management-, scientific-, and technical-consulting services industry is expected to grow by 83 percent in the next ten years.

- **Geriatric health care.** The growing population of seniors continues to have a major impact on careers in health care. In the U.S., thirty-four million individuals are 65 years or older, and that population will double by 2030. About eight out of ten seniors have at least one chronic health condition, and about 50 percent have at least two. As the numbers of aging baby boomers increase, so does the demand for certain health-care jobs and services, including nursing, personal care, and home health care.

- **Mobile media.** Cell phones and other mobile devices are now multifunction devices that enable users to surf the Web, listen to music, download podcasts, use maps, access global-positioning satellites, shoot and send photos and videos, and send text messages. Almost 90 percent of households in the U.S. now have a cell phone. With the countless new software applications, the number of ways to use smart phones is exploding. Analysts predict 24 percent growth for the mobile-media and entertainment industry in 2010.

- **Occupational health and safety.** More specialists are needed to cope with technological advances in safety equipment, changing regulations, and increasing public expectations. The Bureau of Labor Statistics projects 11 percent job growth over the next decade, with six out of ten jobs being in the private sector. Employment growth reflects overall business growth and continuing self-enforcement of government and company regulations.

- **English translation and foreign languages.** In the next 40 years, it is predicted that the number of Spanish-speakers in the United States will rise from thirty-one million to more than one hundred million. For those completely bilingual in Spanish and English, these highly marketable language skills open doors to new careers. The key for language proficiency is to gain experience through practical internships in specialized fields such as law, medicine, and business. Growth for this job field is projected to increase by 22 percent in the coming decade.

- **Renewable energy and the greening of all jobs.** By the mid-twenty-first century, all jobs will be green jobs. Organizations today must address potential regulation changes and look for business-growth opportunities in the new era of sustainable environmental economics. The number of green jobs in the United States grew 9.1 percent between 1998 and

2007—about 250 percent faster than job growth in the economy as a whole, according to a study by The Pew Charitable Trusts. Going green is weighing heavily on consumers' minds, causing them to make daily choices in order to make a difference. According to research from Nielsen, 43 percent of consumers anticipate a greener future within the next five years.

- **Education and training for adults.** Adult education is one of the few industries during a tough economy that has seen positive growth. Job-seekers unable to find employment in their desired fields are going back to school to further their education in other industries. According to the U.S. Bureau of Labor Statistics in 2009, private education was one of only two industries that posted job growth. An increasing number of postsecondary educators are also providing career-related education to working adults. Postsecondary teaching positions are expected to rise by 15 percent in the coming decade.

- **Teaching English as a foreign language.** Half the world's population is expected to be speaking English by 2015. English is a first language for four hundred million people and a fluent second for between three hundred and five hundred million more, according to the International Herald Tribune. Interest in English-teaching positions abroad has mushroomed. This is because English is the international language of business, technology, and academia. College graduates can find teaching jobs abroad, with travel as an added perk.

- **Marine biodiversity and conservation.** Changes in temperature, sea level, and ocean chemistry have enormous implications for marine biodiversity and ecosystem functions. Maintaining the integrity of ocean ecosystems and managing their use in this rapidly changing global environment is one of the greatest challenges of this century. Employment of those in biological sciences is projected to grow 21 percent in the next decade, much faster than the average for all occupations, as biotechnological research and development continues to drive job growth.

- **Health law, international law, intellectual property law.** Employment of lawyers is expected to grow about 14 percent in the coming decade, primarily as a result of growth in the population and in the general level of business activities. Job growth among lawyers also will result from increasing demand for legal services in such areas as health care, intellectual property, venture capital, energy, elder, antitrust, and environmental law. Take health law as one example. Legal and medical experts agree that health law is one of the fastest-growing areas of legal practice. Health-care reform is just one of several reasons for growth in this sector. Additional reasons include more government regulation of health care, the rise of bioethical and biotechnology issues, tort reform related to malpractice, aging of the baby boomer generation, and the consequent growth of Medicare.

- **Action sports innovators.** Job-seekers searching for a strong sector should consider this: Despite the current economic slump, the surf/skate industry has shown notable resiliency during recent global economic challenges, posting U.S. retail sales of $7.22 billion in 2008, according to the Surf Industry Manufacturers Association (SIMA). Although that was down slightly from 2006 ($7.48 billion), the surf industry has shown substantial growth of 10 percent for the past five years.

All these career sectors are being shaped by innovations in science and technology that are being developed daily through universities, labs, and R&D companies across the nation and around the world. Every job within these sectors requires a different level of basic education and/or training as well as a commitment to continuous, recurrent education and training given continuing transformations in technologies and applications in these sectors.

That is why we emphasize the need for all to simultaneously plan for, invest in, and put in place systems that can both rapidly deploy new innovations and build the talent to enable sustainable-growth enterprises.

CHAPTER 3

Keys To Addressing America's Job Gap

A good job and a comfortable lifestyle have been the dream of successive waves of immigrants and migrants. America's history is about the promise of achieving this dream. In this period of massive unemployment and decreasing wage rates, is it time to write an obituary for this dream, or can it still be realized? We clearly believe it can if, as a nation, we focus on the right things.

The red-hot issue in current political discussions is the nationwide call for an economy which produces good jobs for all. The hidden challenge is America's job gap, the disparity between the good jobs already being created and sustained by innovation in the United States, and the lack of American workers with the skills to fill these good jobs. While growing and nurturing innovative American companies is the key to good jobs, without deliberate action, innovation could result in exporting jobs abroad or importing labor while Americans are unemployed or underemployed. The skills of the American workforce are increasingly out of alignment with technological advances required to be globally competitive because of the following:

> **To close America's job gap we need to create and keep good jobs in America by supporting innovative small companies and retraining people to be qualified for new technologies.**

- Most Americans do not have a clear sense of the enormous effects of globalization and new technologies on all industries and all workers and what they must do to be competitive. Even our most educated feel unprepared. While today's university students are extremely concerned with issues of globalization, six out of ten believe their education has not prepared them to address these issues, according to a 2010 IBM survey of 3,600 students.[37]

- The United States is not investing as much money and time in technical-skills development for high school students as other nations. Shortages of skilled workers are acute in many of the world's biggest economies, including the United States and Canada, where employers ranked skilled trades as their number-one or number-two hiring challenge, according to Manpower's 2010 Talent Shortage Survey. "Inadequate training and negative stereotypes relating to skilled trades are further fueling a dangerous shortage of skilled workers," warns Jeffrey A. Joerres, chairman and CEO of Manpower. In its survey of thirty-five thousand employers, "skilled trades" refers to a broad range of job titles that require workers to possess specialized skills, traditionally learned over a period of time as an apprentice. Examples of skilled jobs include: electricians, carpenters, cabinet-makers, masons/bricklayers, plumbers, and welders.[38]

- United States employers do not invest in retraining and upgrading their workers at the levels most European and Asian employers do. U.S. companies have fallen to eighth place for investments in training and employee development, as ranked by the World Economic Forum in 2009.[39]

- Our free-market economy, while tremendously successful at stimulating entrepreneurship and innovation, has been less adept at assuring our talent pool is ready for new technologies and market opportunities. Employers' perceptions of employment readiness are not good. Business journalist Katherine Hughes notes, "From companies like Cisco Systems and Manpower to the Bill and Melinda Gates Foundation, American businesses and business leaders are spending millions of dollars to address what they perceive to be a deficiency in the ability of the American education system to adequately prepare students to meet the demands of the workplace of the early twenty-first century."[40] International test scores bear this out. Compared with their peers in Europe and Asia, 15-year-olds in the United States are below average in applying math and science skills to real-life tasks, according to the Paris-based Organization for Cooperation and Development, which develops yearly rankings for thirty industrialized nations.[41]

America is also losing its way because the general public still believes that the future of its economy is going to be in big companies and in finding the next General Motors, General Electric, or General Mills. It is not the 'Generals' who will solve our problems; it's the privates! The real opportunities are coming from small, private companies. San Diego, for example, witnessed this organic phenomenon with the growth of both wireless IT and the life-sciences clusters that sprang up adjacent to the University of California, San Diego. As a consequence, the region experienced a 4.3-percent increase in median household income from 2000 to 2008, according to a Brookings Institution study,[42] when overall comparable metropolitan regions experienced a 1.7-percent decline, and the nation as a whole, a 4.1-percent decline. Regions that continue to grow innovative clusters and retrain workers in new and converging technologies such as clean technology, health-care IT, and biofuels will be prosperous in the future.

To close America's job gap we need to create and keep good jobs in America by supporting innovative small companies and retraining people to be qualified for new technologies. The time has come to sync training with innovation to get ahead of the curve. Machinists who once worked in auto plants need to be reskilled for wind energy. Medical workers skilled in high-touch fields need to operate high-tech devices so health care can go digital. As countless jobs go green, all Americans need to learn how to run a planet-sustaining economy.

We need to support innovative small companies that create good jobs and we need to retrain our workers to be qualified in new skills so we don't have to export jobs or import labor. The American dream of good jobs for all depends on it.

WHAT IS SHAPING THE JOB GAP

Whether you are a policymaker, entrepreneurial job creator, or simply an individual exploring career options, it is critical to understand the transformative effects of technological advances and global market shifts on local (not just national) economic horizons. Accelerating and nurturing innovative enterprises and knowing how to recognize and engage the innovations that are likely to transform the content of existing work or give rise to job opportunities is the key to both individual and community prosperity. Just as important, Americans need to move away from the idea that they can rely upon or are entitled to one job for a lifetime, and learn how to adapt to continuous shifts in knowledge and skill requirements.

A NEW MINDSET

Connecting innovation, job opportunities, and prosperity requires a mindset that differs from how people thought about and planned for economic growth and prosperity during America's agricultural and industrial eras. When natural resources and manufacturing outputs were the key drivers of wealth and job creation, scale, routinization, and increasing specialization were essential to both the content of work and the organization of productive activity. In the knowledge age, experimentation, innovation, early market penetration, and increasingly shorter times to product obsolescence are what drive growth. In this type of world, smaller entities become the centers of work and the skill requirements change continually. Adaptability, educability, and mobility become the essential ingredients of workforce success.

In many ways, robust clusters of small enterprises are assuming the role that large, vertically integrated companies played in the industrial economy. In more and more places, collections of small companies in sectors such as software in Seattle; wireless telephony in San Diego; orthopedic implants in Warsaw, Indiana; sporting goods in Los Angeles; or veterinary care in places like Kansas City, Missouri, collectively represent thousands of jobs and billions of dollars in revenues which are equal to or greater than what any one large employer might provide. Nonetheless, most communities and employees long for the big "stable" employer, even though mounting evidence suggests big is not necessarily better.

People still think bigger is better; bigger companies represent more jobs, more profits, more taxes, and a bigger commitment to the community through such things as philanthropy, voluntarism, and community service. Bigger is seen as more stable, less vulnerable to the vagaries of natural disasters, unexpected economic downturns, or shifts in markets. The "bigger is better" attitude extends to the belief that people who lead or rise in big systems are more able, sophisticated, and make better leaders in their communities, as well as their firms. Communities hunger for big companies and lament the absence of "anchor" companies.

In contrast, small is seen as stifling, defying economies of scale, and limiting personal growth and advancements. Small is not capable of creating significant profits, jobs, or other forms of civic value. The truth is, big companies in the knowledge age only can remain competitive by improving productivity (aka, downsizing) and by staying close to key markets (aka, globalizing), so at a certain point all big companies stop growing jobs. In contrast, innovation—now the purview of small companies—is creating new markets, not just new products. Such enterprises need lots of talent to grow jobs quickly. The take-home lesson here is to look to the small, the innovative, the sometimes-risky options, not just the supposedly "stable" employers.

INNOVATORS CREATE NEW JOBS SO THEY NEED OUR SUPPORT

In America, close to half of the companies on today's Fortune 500 list did not exist twenty-five years ago, and the number of companies from Brazil, India, China, and Russia on the Financial Times 500 list more than quadrupled in the period from 2006 to 2008 (from 15 to 62). In less than two decades, technologies such as the Web, gene therapy, algae biofuels, biodegradable components of automobiles, and wireless health are driving the development of entirely new industry sectors that promise good jobs for welders and pipefitters, accountants and technicians—not just engineers, biochemists, and managers. Do we as a nation have the skill-ready workforce to seize these opportunities? Are you as an individual ready to pursue a high-paying job, even a career, in one of these globally competitive sectors?

The numbers say it all. In the fall of 2009, the Small Business Administration (SBA) in the United States Department of Commerce reported that small firms (500 persons or fewer) employ more than 50 percent of Americans, account for the lion's share of net new jobs in America, and generate thirteen times more patents per employee than large firms. The SBA data is summarized in the chart reproduced below in Figure 9.

Figure 9

How important are small businesses to the U.S. economy?

Small firms:

- Represent 99.7 percent of all employer firms.
- Employ just over half of all private sector employees.
- Pay 44 percent of total U.S. private payroll.
- Have generated 64 percent of net new jobs over the past 15 years.
- Create more than half of the nonfarm private gross domestic product (GDP).
- Hire 40 percent of high tech workers (such as scientists, engineers, and computer programmers).
- Are 52 percent home-based and 2 percent franchises.
- Made up 97.3 percent of all identified exporters and produced 30.2 percent of the known export value in FY 2007.
- Produce 13 times more patents per employee than large patenting firms; these patents are twice as likely as large firm patents to be among the one percent most cited.

Source: U.S. Dept. of Commerce, Bureau of the Census and International Trade Admin.; Advocacy-funded research by Kathryn Kobe, 2007 (www.sba.gov/advo/research/rs299tot.pdf) and CHI Research, 2003 (www.sba.gov/advo/research/rs225tot.pdf); U.S. Dept. of Labor, Bureau of Labor Statistics.

If America continues to invest in basic research and technology development at the increasing levels needed to fuel successful innovation, then we will see major growth and expansion in industries such as digital-media arts; biotech and life sciences applications in agriculture; health and renewable energy; health-care management and delivery; data mining; leisure and hospitality; adult education and training services; wireless applications and services. The list could go on and on. What all the growth sectors share is the fact that innovation—the creative application of new technologies and techniques to products and services for which there are markets—is driving their growth.

That growth depends on talent skilled in the technologies and practices that enable the growth and global competitiveness of these sectors. This is why we need to be investing in developing the skills necessary to successfully deploy emerging technologies and practices, while simultaneously investing in the development of the innovative technologies themselves. The wealth of our nation and the prosperity of the American workforce comes from the successful deployment of inventions—not from the inventions themselves. By keeping track of where R&D is going, which applications are being commercialized, and in what sectors new start-up companies are proliferating, it is possible to anticipate where the jobs may be and identify the skills they will likely require. Then America can begin preparing people through education and training so they are ready when the demand for workers accelerates. In this way, we can minimize the need to import labor or export jobs in new technology sectors.

INNOVATIVE COMPANIES REQUIRE NEW SKILLS

Innovation has two important effects on the job horizons shaping America's future. Innovation can transform the content of existing jobs in the way computer manufacturing has transformed the factory floor, e-marketing has changed sales, and the way laparoscopic technology has changed major surgical practices and composite materials (the content of sporting equipment such as golf clubs and surfboards). Innovation can also give rise to breakthrough technologies which create new industry sectors and radically new skill requirements, the way breakthroughs in molecular biology, gene therapy, and monoclonal antibodies have created new drug-development companies, clinical-research organizations, and biotech manufacturing with all the attendant regulatory, legal, accounting, marketing, sales, and management functions. Similarly, the explosion of wireless telephony (cell phones), over the last two decades, has resulted in entire new industries that provide wireless applications from GPS to online news services to restaurant reservations.

The skills required by these and countless new knowledge-based sectors are not reflected in the content of the typical community-college curriculum or government-funded training programs, which, for the most part, are still captive of the old-economy companies and job skills—the flat or declining job sectors. What is needed is a much closer alignment between public innovation investments in R&D and commercialization and the education-and-training priorities of the publicly funded talent-development system. What is needed for individuals who seek to find or plan to keep employment is continuous education and reeducation in the new technologies, organizational skills, and market strategies required by American companies to remain globally competitive.

ADAPTABILITY IS THE KEY TO SUSTAINABILITY

In a supplement on Innovation in Emerging Economies (China, India, Brazil) in an April 2010 issue of *The Economist*, the importance of adaptability is dramatically demonstrated. Countries once seen as sources of cheap labor or easy markets for American products are redefining innovation processes. They are reengineering how products are manufactured and marketed in a manner that is not only suitable to their economic circumstances and population trends, but in ways that challenge the conventional wisdom and practices of the allegedly more "advanced" West, be it in accessible consumer products or in technology-intensive products such as cell phones, automobiles, or hand-held electrocardiogram devices. *The Economist* notes that developing countries are becoming hotbeds of business innovation in much the same way as Japan did from the 1950s onward. They are coming up with new products and services that are dramatically cheaper than their Western equivalents: $3,000 cars, $300 computers, and $30 mobile phones that provide nationwide service for just two cents a minute. They are reinventing systems of production and distribution, and they are experimenting with entirely new business models. All the elements of modern business, from supply-chain management to recruitment and retention, are being rejigged or reinvented in one emerging market or another. Local companies in the developing world are "dreaming bigger dreams," according to *The Economist*, at the same time that they are substantially increasing their investments in research, as well as technical and higher education.

The growth of their economic and innovation capacity as well as the enormous size of their markets means "rethinking everything from products to distribution systems"—and not just within developing countries. Multinationals, according to *The Economist*, expect as much as 70 percent of the world's growth to come from emerging markets, with 50 percent coming from China and India. These developments represent enormous challenges and opportunities for American companies and workers. They will not be opportunities, however, unless we all adapt, quickly and continuously. [43]

INNOVATORS AND TALENT SUSTAINING COMMUNITIES

Given the forces of globalization and transformative technologies, one of the central questions for our nation is: What is America's role in the world? For individuals, this issue translates into: What is my role in the American economy? Assuming that our shared goal is a vibrant and prosperous economy capable of supporting good jobs for all, it is important to address what strategies are most likely to assure the realization of this goal. Recent federal initiatives to rescue America from the brink of a depression have buoyed major industries, such as automobile manufacturing, and stabilized global financial markets. However, they have yet to address our need to accelerate innovation and job readiness simultaneously, in order to assure American citizens can realize employment benefits from start-up and growth companies, and to ensure these companies will not have to export jobs or import labor to realize marketplace success. To do this requires a shift in focus from investments in the "too big to fail" enterprises and systems. Instead, we need to refocus investments in invention, innovation, and growing start-up and growth companies. Simultaneously, we need a major investment in retooling, reskilling, and upgrading the competencies of all American workers, including welders, engineers, nurses, teachers, biochemists, and executives.

The growth strategy for the United States, as well as the best strategy for employability of individuals, is to focus on two things. The first is a growing regional innovation capacity so that communities can continually renew their economic base through new growth technologies and companies that fill the gaps created by declining technologies and companies. The second is assuring regional workforces are "ready" to engage or adapt to the skills and knowledge required to support emerging and growth companies as the job opportunities in stable and declining industries diminish. This, in turn, means concentrating on where new ideas are coming from—especially R&D activities in universities and companies at home and abroad; increasing public and private investments in entrepreneurial knowledge-based enterprises; supporting the work of regional intermediaries focused on linking research, commercialization, and workforce-development activities; and investing in education and training relevant to the knowledge and competencies regional-growth industries require. These investments will enable the kind of adaptability and nimbleness both local communities and individual citizens need to remain competitive in a rapidly changing global community.

FINAL THOUGHTS

Closing America's job gap is as much about changing attitudes and world view as it is about putting more time and money into companies and people. We must stop putting time and money into buoying up industries based on declining technologies, organizations ill-equipped to respond rapidly to global changes and opportunities, or education and training programs disconnected from the skills and knowledge essential to the success of startup and growth companies; doing so will continue to erode our competitiveness in the world and prosperity at home. The good news is that there are already lots of jobs out there for enterprising people who go after the training they need to qualify for those jobs. Chapter IV provides a number of encouraging examples.

CHAPTER 4

Opportunities for Job and Career Seekers

There is much that needs to be done at the public-policy level and within educational institutions to narrow the gap between the jobs that are being transformed or created and the skills of the American workforce (which we address at the end of this book). Nonetheless, Americans interested in a good job do not need to wait for solutions from policymakers, training companies, or business owners. There is much that can be done right now. What does the job gap mean for the individual who wants to get a good job in an innovative economy?

The following are sixteen sectors of the economy that offer opportunities for good jobs. In some of the profiles we have included, actual stories of individuals who have bridged to new careers in areas of higher demand (pulled from the authors' experience as educators in the continuing-education division of UC San Diego). The common thread running through the information is that the key to a good job is acquiring the knowledge necessary to make the transition. The chapter ends with research from the gatekeepers of the good jobs (i.e., the employers) on what they are looking for today from potential employees.

HOT CAREER SECTORS

1. Health-Information Technology

When a patient visits a hospital, the staff creates a detailed medical report. Whether the condition is severe (e.g., a heart attack or a broken arm) or a routine checkup, the patient's details are documented. This medical record also contains all the physician's notes, X-rays, lab results, recommended treatment plans, and current medications.

Health-information technicians are responsible for organizing these medical records, ensuring that the charts are accurate and complete. These technicians also update patients' files electronically.[44]

In the past, all medical records were kept as paper documents stored in file cabinets. Reports were cumbersome to access. Information could not be easily shared, and files could be misplaced or lost. Yet, this was the medical filing system for millions of patients across the U.S.

Due to government initiatives in recent years, the health-care industry adopted an advanced technology system for managing and utilizing health information.[45] With this national initiative, medical establishments have the goal of transferring all health-care information to an advanced technology-driven database within the next decade. This is fueling a demand for health-information technicians who can support medical-record reform.[46]

As technology increases, so does the need for health-information technicians to use and maintain patient data that is vital for quality health care and to keep all medical records organized and confidential. Electronic health records (EHR) will continue to expand to include patient data from various sources (eventually integrating text, voice, images, and handwritten notes).[47]

Technicians are needed for emerging jobs such as health care integration engineer, health care systems analyst, clinical IT consultant, and technology support specialist. Jobs and needs in the health care information technology field are a critical component of plans for positive change in the health care industry.[48]

Technicians are needed for emerging jobs such as health-care-integration engineer, health-care systems analyst, clinical IT consultant, and technology support specialist. Jobs and needs in the health-care information-technology field are a critical component of plans for positive change in the health-care industry.[49]

Job prospects for the health-information technology industry should be very good, according to the Bureau of Labor Statistics, and are expected to grow faster than average.

"Several factors—a growing industry with vast employment needs, a societal concern with federal backing for broad reform, and a solution incorporating advanced knowledge and skills among workers—combine to form a strong base for workforce development and employment opportunity for the coming decade," notes Mark Cafferty, San Diego Workforce Partnership president and CEO.

"The injection of skilled knowledge workers into the magnet of health-care information technology will not only provide solutions to immediate needs, but also will serve as a catalyst for new and emerging types of jobs in the coming years as the impact of health-care IT takes hold."[50]

According to the Bureau of Labor Statistics, medical records and health-information technicians held about 172,500 jobs in 2008 (about 39 percent of jobs were in hospitals). Jobs are expected to grow by 20 percent, or about 35,100 new jobs, for the decade 2008–2018. Health-information technicians work with a number of health-care providers, such as physician offices, nursing care facilities, outpatient care centers, and home-health-care services. Technicians also may be employed outside of health-care facilities, such as at federal-government agencies.[51]

Jean's Story

As a registered nurse, Jean Frazier has worked in labor and delivery for eight years. Now, she is helping to usher in a new era in health care: information technology.

"I have always been very interested in the use of technology in the health-care industry," Frazier says. "The first hospital I worked at in Louisiana was doing paper charting. They tried to implement information technology with computer charting, but they didn't provide the proper education for the staff and they didn't really get people on board with it before implementation. It was rejected by the nurses after several months, so we went back to paper. I was very interested in the hospital going electronic because I saw the advantages of it, including cutting down overtime for the nurses."

When Frazier moved to San Diego six years ago to work as an RN at UC San Diego Medical Center, she helped the other nurses at that hospital get up to speed on the new bar-coding technology for medications.

"Every time you introduce something new to a hospital, like technology, it can be challenging because the nurses feel overworked, and they often feel they don't have the support they need," Frazier explains.

Frazier decided that the only way she could effectively ease nurses and physicians into the digital age was to learn more about information technology. That's when she took the UC San Diego Extension Health Care IT program, which examines the impact of health-care IT on different health-care environments and organizations, as well as the national implications of effective implementation.

"We received an overview of the health-care system in a way I had never learned as a bedside nurse, like content-management systems, how billing works, and how IT fits into the hospital," Frazier recalls about the Extension program. "We also learned about networking and computers and the different applications being used in health care, as well as how national policy impacts health-care IT.

"The course gave me an understanding of what I could do within the health-care information-technology field," she adds. "Everybody in the course was so different—from project managers to clinicians to technical writers—and it was great to see how each has a place to fit into this health-care IT field. This field is still emerging, so a lot of people don't know what kinds of jobs are available. What the course afforded was the opportunity to understand what heath-care IT is about and how I fit into it with my particular skill set and interests."

Frazier, who completed the Extension course in March 2010, recently started a new job using her newfound health-care IT skills. As a senior specialist in evidence-based medicine for Sharp HealthCare, she acts as a liaison between the hospital's IT department and the clinicians and helps transfer medical records from paper to electronic versions.

Frazier said information technology not only improves efficiency for hospitals but also increases safety for patients.

"With electronic medical records I can now easily and quickly read what a physician has entered into the computer about a patient instead of needing to spend time clarifying what they have written by hand," she explains. "As a nurse, I now have access to many aspects of that patient's record, regardless of where I am in the hospital. So I'm not waiting on a paper chart that someone else is using. I have immediate access to the patient's information. With technology, like bar coding—where you can scan the barcodes to cross reference a patient's wristband with his or her medication—you can cut down on the potential errors of giving that patient the wrong medication.

"There are also reminders we can set in the programs that pop up on a computer that tell us when a patient is due for a wellness or follow-up exam," she adds. "Before, we had to sort through paper records. Information technology gives us a much more efficient way to know about and follow the care of a patient."

While Frazier hasn't been in her new job long, she is already hopeful for her future career and for the future of the health-care industry as it embraces information technology as the standard practice of patient care.

"My initial passion for being an RN was assisting women through the labor and delivery process; you're supporting someone and making the process as easy and pleasant as possible," she reveals. "That's still my focus. I want to help the transition to information technology in health care be as easy and efficient as possible and make our health-care system even safer and more pleasant for the patients."

2. Clinical Trials Design and Management for Oncology

Biopharmaceutical drug companies have more than doubled investments in research and development in the last decade. Annual sales in the worldwide pharmaceutical market are estimated to more than double by 2020 to $1.3 trillion. [52]

This increase is partially due to an aging and sedentary population. As the population ages, diseases are becoming more prevalent.[53] In addition, new markets for therapeutic and curative drugs are opening in developing countries. To better manage how drugs are developed and brought to market, employees are needed to manage and design clinical trials, in particular, trials testing new cancer drugs.[54]

Currently, it takes an average of twelve years for an experimental drug to be approved and brought to market. Researchers must screen thousands of compounds to obtain a handful of drug candidates that will enter preclinical testing in animals and advance to clinical testing in humans. The odds of any new drug making it through to market are slim—about one in five thousand. With a long lag time to market and sometimes billions of dollars in expenses, this business plan is costly, laborious, and ineffective. The industry requires innovation to remain viable.[55]

Pharmaceutical companies also face other external pressures. These include less revenue as patents expire on existing blockbuster drugs, fewer new drugs in the pipeline, and increased marketing and regulatory expenses.

In general, returns on pharmaceutical stocks are lagging behind other industries. For example, the Dow Jones World Index during the past few years rose about 35 percent, while the FTSE Global Pharmaceuticals Index rose just over 1 percent.[56]

Clinical trials are conducted in hospitals and medical clinics. These trials test whether a new drug or treatment has a beneficial result when compared to an existing treatment or a placebo. Testing has three stages: Phase I, Phase II, and Phase III. Phase I trials are the initial clinical trials in humans. The major objective of a Phase I trial is to evaluate the safety of a new treatment measuring toxicity and side effects.

Phase II trials determine whether the new treatment is effective and warrants further study. Phase III trials are confirmatory studies that typically assign patients to treatment groups. The goal of Phase III is to compare a new treatment to the current best treatment or other control group.[57]

At the heart of any clinical study is proving and confirming the safety and efficacy of the tested drug. This is true for both general therapeutics and, more specifically, for oncology studies.

How do scientists find better ways to treat cancer and improve the overall standard of cancer care? Current cancer therapeutics and recent advances have prompted changes in the design and conduct of oncology clinical trials. As cancer treatments improve and survival rates for many types of cancer increase, drug developers need to adjust their methodologies and metrics to account for the new statistics.[58]

Two goals exist in cancer trials: to determine an optimal dose and find safe treatment for the individual patient. Oncology Phase I trials determine the drug's safety profile, including the safe-dosage range, or the maximum tolerated dose (MTD). Phase I also looks at how the drug is absorbed, distributed, metabolized, and excreted (ADME). Phase II determines the efficacy of the MTD by measuring the complete and partial radiography responses. Phase III confirms Phase II findings on a larger scale with more varied treatment groups.[59]

The challenges of oncology clinical-trial designs are constantly being evaluated. These include: choosing the appropriate dosage, managing data complexity, designing a treatment plan, overcoming operational challenges, implementing safety requirements, and recruiting patients.[60]

3. Data Mining

Looking for a needle in a haystack is a good analogy for data-mining jobs. Data mining is the technique of extracting specific types of information or patterns from large databases, such as data warehouses.

Very advanced statistical methods are used to sift through large volumes of data for analysis, providing answers to questions that were once too time-consuming. It has great potential to help businesses predict future trends and behaviors so that they can make better business and knowledge-driven decisions.[61]

Data-mining analysts are responsible for conducting this type of valuable research for industry and government agencies, and career prospects in this industry are bright. Most businesses in every industry collect data, and in the digital age, information is crucial for success. For example, retailers want to know which consumers are using what kinds of products and services.[62]

The data-mining analyst uses all available historical purchasing be-haviors to create a model that predicts which customers would likely re-spond to a new product. The results allow the retailer to directly market to those specific customers, ensuring that the appropriate individuals re-ceive promotional offers tailored to their buying habits.

The Federal Bureau of Investigation uses data mining for security and intelligence screening. Algorithms and regression analysis are used to identify potentially illegal or incriminating electronic information that is distributed over the Internet.[63]

Additional data-mining-industry applications include:

- A pharmaceutical company can analyze its sales activity to im-prove targeting high-value physicians by determining which marketing activities will have the greatest impact.

- A credit-card company can leverage its vast warehouse of cus-tomer-transaction data to identify customers most likely to be interested in a new credit product.

- A diversified transportation company with a large direct-sales force can apply data mining to identify the best prospects for its services.

- A large consumer packaged-goods company can apply data mining to improve its sales process to retailers.

Data-mining technology can be applied to any business that wants to leverage information to improve business. Information can be used to learn about customers, reduce costs, and improve efficiencies. It can help companies focus their marketing strategies, so they can appeal to selected customers and know how to reach them.[64]

More important, data mining is a rapidly growing industry due to the explosion of available data. A study by students and faculty at UC Berke-ley found that the amount of data in the world doubles every three years. For this reason, more employees are needed in the data-mining industry to drill down, analyze, and interpret the data.[65]

Career prospects exist in several areas, including advertising technology, fraud detection, surveillance, Web mining, probabilistic trading, risk management, business intelligence, scientific research, and law enforcement. Data mining requires comprehension of algorithms and advanced statistics, and the ability to program and use advanced software. Job-hunters with computer-science and statistics training, along with good business sense, would be well suited to this career. Individuals with an understanding of the appropriate math and computer science would also be well qualified.[66]

Data-mining analysts, data-mining researchers, data-mining scientists, and other data-mining professionals can expect to earn high wages.[67]

Peter's Story

Fresh from a presentation to secure a data-mining project, Peter Chen is delighted anew with his decision to go for certification in the emerging discipline of searching reams of information to look for better answers from a bigger picture.

"Having a data-mining certificate certainly not only opens up the opportunity for this project, but also adds credibility to my presentation as the sole data-mining consultant for that segment of the proposal," Chen reveals. "Both the skills and the certificate have been incredibly useful in my new consulting position. I'm working on multiple projects now and I've got requests for proposals that have the potential to be very interesting."

Chen was downsized out of a company last year where he'd worked in informatics and finance for several years.

Ironically, his previous employer paid for his continuing education at a university in data mining, then sent him out on his own, where he is finding plenty of work.

"Downsizing worked out for me," Chen admits. "I'm working several levels higher now."

Data mining is a collection of tools and techniques to sift the biggest picture possible for clues to how things work and how they could be better. There's so much information now that has been stored in databases or database-friendly formats since computers made their way into our workplaces, our record-keeping, our calendars, and even our shopping carts.

Data mining aims to develop or create algorithms that tell us what our information means. eHarmony's matchmaking and Google's method for ranking search results are widely used data-mining examples. But finding meaning and revelations in data has spread far wider, from insurance actuaries to transportation scheduling to how to deliver effective community health care, based on what has actually happened.

"Data mining is a powerful tool for predictive problem solving," Chen notes. "People see it as a magic black box: "I put stuff in and stuff comes out," but it doesn't really work that way. There's a lot more to it."

One of the biggest challenges is making the data usable. Strange as that sounds, think of the different methods of entering a date into an Excel spreadsheet. It can be entered month-day-year, day-month-year, and even year-month-day, in the method of some invoicing. And it can be stored so the computer recognizes it as text, as a date, or as numbers that can be added and subtracted. How a single agency saves its data and what program it has used can span twenty-five years of changes and a dozen iterations.

"If you do have the data you need, it's often very dirty," Chen says. "A big part of each project is cleaning up the data and making it usable, and being sure you've gotten rid of data that is full of mistakes. Since a lot of it is legacy data, that's often much of the work."

Once the data can be worked, the data miner turns to problem-mapping, devising and documenting protocols for searching the data to get usable results. There are usually several different ways to do that.

"A lot of people jam it all in and see what comes out," Chen reveals. "But you want to get a meaningful result and that means looking at the best data of the relevant variables."

With a bachelor's degree from the Massachusetts Institute of Technology, Chen worked in predictive and quantitative modeling in the financial sector.

Chen began the five-class, five-quarter data-mining program in 2008, studying advanced techniques for preparing data and using sophisticated software programs that support handling millions of records.

"The classes are online, so you can be anywhere and take them at a time that works for you," Chen notes. "We had video lectures and problem sets each week to work on."

Fortunately, Chen felt like he had plenty of opportunities to interact with his instructors.

"The Extension's instructors were Ph.D.s who work in the industry, so you learn what happens in real life," Chen says. "They gave us different projects that were culled from real projects so we learned a lot about the real challenges and rewards."

Data-mining students worked on the most prominent open-source software, WEKA, which has both point-and-click and script-writing in its applications, allowing for very in-depth and quirky searches.

"The results are often surprising and can change the way people are thinking about solving problems," Chen tells us. "The question you have at the start isn't necessarily the question you'll find you actually want the answer to. That's one indication that you've done it correctly."

4. Embedded Engineering

We live in a digital-technology world where just about everyone owns or uses a device that contains a microchip processor. Devices from phones, appliances, and televisions to automobiles and iPods all use processors to run. These complex digital processors, or computers, are embedded systems—often built around a microprocessor core—that are designed by software engineers.

Embedded systems perform a specific task. They are often located in the controlled device, have operational software with read-only memory, and function with limited user interaction. The systems are used both in very simple products, such as electronic greeting cards and toys, and very complex and powerful devices,[68] including entertainment devices, health-care equipment, automotive items, mobile phones, and avionics.

Embedded engineers are deeply involved in creating this complex technology. Embedded engineers are multidisciplinary specialists, bridging the gap between software and hardware design. They have a broad background in electric engineering and computer science (EECS). They also manage projects of various complexities in target systems.[69]

Most companies hire embedded engineers who have at least a bachelor's degree. Candidates must also have a broad knowledge of, and experience with, a variety of computer systems and technologies. The most common majors are applications hardware/software engineering, computer science, mathematics, computer engineering, communications, networking, control systems, and other technical disciplines. Graduate degrees are preferred for some of the more complex jobs.[70]

According to the Bureau of Labor Statistics, software engineers can expect rapid employment growth, with an additional 295,200 software engineer jobs between 2008 and 2018. Overall, software-engineering jobs are expected to increase by 32 percent, one of the highest rates for all occupations.[71]

With the continuing convergence of communication and computing functions within devices, embedded systems are becoming more complex. More-powerful processors and peripherals are in continuous demand. This rapid growth in technology has led to significant skills shortages in the embedded-systems field of engineering. Embedded systems are literally everywhere. Graduates are likely to be employed in a diverse range of industries with above-average salaries compared to traditional software engineers.[72]

Bill's Story

When layoffs and cutbacks hit SpaceDev, Inc. in 2009, Bill Jackson says his newly acquired knowledge of embedded engineering may have helped him keep his job.

"There's no question that the guy who can do five things is harder to get rid of than the guy who can only do one or two," Jackson says. "The more diverse your toolset, the more stable your job will be."

Even with 25 years of experience as an aerospace engineer, a Ph.D. in engineering, a senior post as engineer supervisor at the company, based in Poway, California, and a laundry list of successful projects behind him, Jackson still wasn't guaranteed a job after SpaceDev was bought by Sierra Nevada Corporation last year. "Aerospace is a notoriously unstable industry," Jackson reveals. "You understand that if you last long enough."

Jackson, now working in Colorado, didn't know that any particular changes were coming when he tackled a two-and-a-half-year program to earn a professional certificate in embedded engineering. He just knew that he wanted to understand his staff better.

"A significant portion of my job involves working with and supervising people who develop complex embedded systems on satellites. I work on the pointy end of the rocket," Jackson explains. "All the younger guys had been exposed to embedded systems in school and I've been out for twenty-five years. There was no such thing as embedded systems when I went to engineering school." That meant he didn't understand some of the finer points of what he was watching them do, and that made Jackson uncomfortable.

"You watch people working and you're wondering, why is he doing it that way; how does that work? And, worst of all, I had to make critical design decisions on things I didn't fully understand."

He looked around and found a continuing-education certificate program, and liked that it is being taught by working embedded-engineering professionals. Tony Babian, who is the assistant director of engineering programs at UC San Diego Extension, says the university launched the certificate program at the beginning of the millennium.

"SPAWAR, the Navy's high-tech procurement arm, and Qualcomm send their employees to our certificate program," Babian says. "We have people who have masters and Ph.D.s in engineering who attend."

Babian notes that the range of students is across the board—from college students earning credits to people like the Canadian executive who is taking the class online now because, as the manager of embedded engineering at a Canadian company, he'd like to understand what his staff is doing.

Jackson took a total of ten classes at the university—seven online and three in the classroom. "A lot of the classes involved hands-on miniature projects of what you would do in the real world," he says. Jackson found the online courses, with regular assignments to be turned in, Webinar-style lectures, and exercises within each week's lesson, more challenging than being in a classroom in some ways.

"You have to be really motivated to make the time and get things done on time for each class, because there is no regularly scheduled meeting with an instructor and a room full of students."

But it also has its upside. "I work long hours and sometimes have to travel a lot on my job," Jackson reveals. I can grab my laptop and chip away at the course from my hotel room."

Aerospace is an inherently unstable profession that floats on big-dollar government contracts, and just a few big companies do much of the work—and hiring. Jackson has survived downturns and layoffs before, and he wasn't surprised when tough economic times resulted in his company being sold.

"Last year, when we were bought by Sierra Nevada and they figured out what I do, they asked me to move to Colorado," Jackson divulges. "I'm pretty sure that being current on embedded engineering and being willing to learn job skills on my own helped me survive the acquisition."

The company moved Jackson and his family to Colorado, where they now live minutes outside of Boulder. "We've always wanted to live here, so it's a great opportunity," Jackson says. "And it's really nice to have a job in this economy."

Although the classes were tough, Jackson claims it was worth the effort and expense. "Any money you invest in yourself is money well spent," he says. "It gives you something no one can take away from you: knowledge and skill, and the confidence that comes from adapting to an ever-changing business environment."

5. Feature Writing for the Web

Web/online journalism refers to news content reported, produced, and distributed via the Internet. According to University of Southern California's Annenberg Center for the Digital Future 2009 Annual Report, online-newspaper Web site readership is the highest ever. The center found Internet users are reading online newspapers for fifty-three minutes per week, up from forty-one minutes the prior year.[73]

"For the first time in sixty years, newspapers are back in the breaking-news business," reports center director Jeffrey Cole, "except now, their delivery method is electronic and not paper. On the Web, newspapers are live, and they can supplement their coverage with audio, video, and the invaluable resources of their vast archives. And, they already have talented teams of reporters and editors who can deliver the news."[74]

These are exciting times for news journalism reported on the Web. The technology has transformed journalism, creating new ways for news to be reported, delivered, and read. The new medium also allows for much more interactivity, as readers respond via comments or blogs. Web/online journalists have the opportunity to shape the future.[75]

To be sure, the journalism industry is currently in flux. Traditional newspapers have seen massive layoffs in recent years, while many new online publications still struggle in the start-up phase. The number-one question that remains for both veteran and aspiring journalists alike is: What technological skills do I need to stay relevant and employed?

And the answer?

"Well, it's the same one I gave some ten years ago" says Robert Hernandez of Online Journalist Review. "Know journalism."[76]

A journalistic career usually starts with a bachelor's degree in journalism or mass communications. Liberal-arts courses in English, writing, sociology, political science, history, economics, and psychology provide exposure to a broad knowledge base for aspiring journalists.[77] Additional skills a journalist needs to develop are in mass media, basic reporting, copyediting, journalist ethics, and broadcasting. Elective courses in foreign language, computer science, and business may also be helpful.[78]

In general, journalism is a competitive field, and the skills required for a Web journalist are similar, but with a technology spin. These skills are: good, solid news judgment; strong morals and ethics; an ability to meet deadlines; and a mastery of The Associated Press Stylebook. Additional Web skills include knowledge of HTML, a working understanding of Search Engine Optimization (SEO), social-media literacy, and the willingness to try new technologies. Web journalists combine these skills to tell stories in all media: text, photos, audio, video, and a combination of all four.[79]

The best Web journalists succeed in the industry going beyond mere reporting and building a person brand. These reporters create value around their individual work, so that employers will want to keep them and readers will want to keep following their work. Savvy journalists also promote their stories on Facebook and other social-media sites. Web writers know that when their name is valuable to the public, they become more valuable to employers, investors, and advertisers.[80]

Nikki's Story

Nikki Li always loved visual arts and the stories that come with it, but her continuing education at a college allowed her to begin to make art and make a living simultaneously in a way that makes her far happier than cataloging and curating.

"It made me realize that I'd rather be doing my own creative things instead of curating other peoples', though I do continue to enjoy art," she reveals. "But I fit better in an atmosphere where I'm creative and I work as my own boss than I did when I worked at museums."

As her own boss, running Akula Kreative, she builds Web sites, creates brochures, works with clients on branding and creating logos, and helps with search engine optimization, among myriad other tasks.

It's a big change from the path she was on, and Li says she's happy about that. Li graduated with a degree in art history from Vassar College in 2004.

"I thought I'd like to work in a museum or a gallery," she recalls. After a stint at the Lux Art Institute in Encinitas, California, Li landed a position at the Getty Museum in Los Angeles as a senior assistant to the curator of the manuscripts department, and she enjoyed the job . . . for a while. "I started to get restless and bored, and I started trying to think of what else I'd like to do," she remembers. "It was bad enough that I left the job and came back to San Diego to think about what I wanted to do next."

Li found a continuing-education certificate program in graphic and Web design, a one-year course of five classes on how to use the latest tools to build Web sites as well as create brochures and logos, and on how to find and keep customers.

"I was worried when I signed up because I didn't have any computer skills, like Adobe Photoshop and Dreamweaver," she confesses, mentioning the very popular graphic- design and Web site–building software. "But there was room for someone starting at the absolute beginning."

Li worked energetically at her program. "I'd say 50 percent of my success is what I learned in class and 50 percent was from my own research. I really liked the projects I worked on as assignments and I put a lot of extra effort into them to learn as much as I could. I made a point of getting as much as I could out of each class."

Li liked that the program focused more on design than on programming. "I didn't expect to know everything about Web design. We did a tremendous amount of work learning the most current programs and learning about resources to keep up with them as they evolve and update," she says.

She completed her courses in 2009, earning a certificate that gave her extra confidence when it came to starting her own business. "I work with a lot of different clients on a lot of different projects, from small businesses in the start-up stages to well-established businesses adding an Internet component. I have a wide variety of projects, so I don't get bored with what I'm doing."

Li likes working for herself. She notes that she spends a lot less time doing administrative work now, and she has been able to streamline her company's internal processes so she doesn't have to spend extra time on it, including adding credit-card payments to her billing cycle.

Li notes that a student's commitment is going to be the measure of their success. "Like any class you take, you get as much out of it as you put into it," she says. "I found that there's lots of information out there on how to do specific things, and lots of people willing to help you understand how to accomplish what you set out to do."

6. Geriatric Health Care

The elderly population in the United States is rapidly growing and will have a major impact on families, social services, and the U.S. economy. The increasing need for senior care makes this quite evident. According to the last census in 2000, some fourteen million seniors 65 and older reported some level of disability. Most ailments were related to chronic health conditions, such as heart disease, hypertension, diabetes, arthritis, and respiratory disorders. About 80 percent of seniors have at least one chronic health condition and about 50 percent have at least two.[81]

This increase in the number of seniors accounts for the predicted increase in the geriatric health-care industry and the long-term need for health-care professionals. Geriatric-health-care professionals are dedicated to helping older people stay as healthy and independent as possible.

In the United States, thirty-four million people are 65 years or older, and it is estimated that this population will more than double to seventy million by 2030.[82] Other estimates indicate that by 2050 one out of every five Americans will join the senior population for a total of eighty million people.[83]

Approximately half the people 65 or older live in nine states, led by California, Florida, and New York. The upcoming increases are mainly due to aging of the baby boomer generation: persons born between 1946 and 1964. The demand for home-care services is expected to increase by 50 percent between 2002 and 2012, according to the Bureau of Labor Statistics.[84]

In 2009, Medicare, the U.S. federal government's health-care program, provided for 45.5 million seniors 65 years and older—an increase of $44.8 million from the previous year. By 2030, the number of people covered by Medicare will escalate to about 78 million because of baby boomers entering retirement age.[85]

Other contributing factors are changes in family dynamics. Divorce and fewer children may mean less family support, and assistance may be needed from outside resources, which would increase health-care spending.[86]

According to the U.S. Department of Labor, geriatric health care is one of the fastest-growing sectors of the U.S. economy. The Congressional Budget Office estimates that $135 billion is spent on long-term care for senior citizens.[87] In forty years, women are expected to live to 93, and men, to 86 years of age, an additional eight years longer.

"This will cost the U.S. an additional $8 trillion by the year 2050," reports Dr. Sanjay Gupta of CNN.[88] In 2009, the U.S. hospital-care expenditures were about $789.4 billion, of which nursing-home and in-home health care were $213.6 billion.[89] The geriatric-health-care workforce will require special education and training in caring for older adults, with a focus on preventing and treating disease and disability in later life.[90]

As the U.S. population ages, the number of health-care careers that specifically cater to older persons are increasing. Jobs include attending to seniors, managing facilities, and developing care plans for the elderly. Medical professionals are also in growing demand, including: medical doctors, registered nurses, licensed-practitioner nurses, geriatric nurses, pharmacists, geriatric-care managers, certified home-health aides, certified nursing assistants, and social workers.[91]

7. Mobile Media

Mobile media is a fast-growing trend of the future. It impacts both the young and the old, as cell phones spread in popularity, particularly Web-friendly smart phones.[92]

The latest Business Confidence Index (BCI) from the Mobile Entertainment Forum is projecting a $36 billion mobile-media industry for 2010—a 24-percent growth for the mobile media and entertainment industry. Cell phones and other mobile devices have evolved far beyond answering and sending voice calls. They are now multifunction devices that enable users to surf the Web, listen to music, download podcasts, use maps, access global-positioning satellites, shoot and send photos and videos, and send text messages. With the hundreds of new software applications for phones, the number of ways to use smart phones is exploding.

Every day, the Web is getting faster and easier to use, and is able to access more information. It provides more opportunities for news organizations, the entertainment industry, and advertisers to live stream directly to cell phones.[93] Graphic designers, videographers, video editors, casual game/app developers, and software engineers are needed to design and develop Web sites and create video content, software applications, games, interfaces, mobile platforms, and more, as demand continues to increase for Web content and next-generation cell phones.

According to the Bureau of Labor Statistics, graphic designers will see a projected increase of 13 percent between the years of 2008 and 2018. An increasing number of graphic designers are needed to develop material for Web pages, interactive media, and multimedia projects.[94]

Employers usually want candidates to have a bachelor's degree in graphic design for most entry-level and advanced graphic-design positions. They will also accept two-year degrees, associate degrees, and certificates in graphic design from continuing-education classes. Individuals who have experience with Web site design and animation will have the best job opportunities.[95]

According to the Bureau of Labor Statistics, software engineers will see an increase of 32 percent, with an expected 295,000 new jobs created between 2008 and 2018—a much greater increase than predicted for other occupations.[96] Massive growth is also expected in mobile video. The BLS predicts more than twenty-three thousand film- and video-editing jobs will be added through the year 2016.

Demand for software engineers will also continue to grow with the evolution of technologies such as the Internet, as well as the increasing number of Web sites, mobile-technology devices, and hand-held computers. These newer technologies, coupled with the expanding number of wireless-Internet regions, have created a demand for new products and mobile applications.[97]

In the United States, 80 percent of adults have cell phones. Of those, 37 percent use their phones to access the Web. About 25 percent acquire some news via cell phone.[98] People digest news and information received via cell phone differently than they do with knowledge acquired on the Web.[99] For example, the *Wall Street Journal* offers downloadable headlines of every article being published. Cell phone subscribers can scan these headlines quickly and choose to read more. When a headline is clicked, a summary opens, giving more description about the story. If they choose, readers can then click to read the full article. These few seconds of navigating and scanning are critical in the mobile-news experience—they determine whether a subscriber turns something off or keeps reading.[100] For graphic designers and software engineers, this means more opportunity for growth in the mobile-media industry.

8. Occupational Health and Safety

"Safety on the job is no accident," goes a popular saying.

Occupational health and safety specialists (OHSS) analyze work environments in order to prevent injury. They are particularly needed in industries involving chemical, physical, and biological agents. The specialist's job is to keep the workplace accident-free by researching safer, healthier, and more-efficient ways of working.

Occupational health and safety experts also analyze and research existing data and other sources to identify trends or patterns of injury or illness. They investigate health-related complaints and inspect facilities to ensure compliance with state and federal laws.[101]

Specialists who work in the biological and chemical industries ensure that chemicals and biological agents are stored and disposed of correctly. They also inspect grounds, checking that protective equipment is available, used properly, and in good working condition.

When incidents do occur, these specialists conduct investigations and shape policies to prevent future accidents or injuries. They also often coordinate rehabilitation for injured employees, to help them return to work. Some specialists develop and implement training programs to improve conditions or practices that have a high risk and are dangerous. They then monitor the progress of the programs.[102]

OHSS work responsibilities vary by industry. Each workplace has a different set of hazards that may affect the safety of its employees. Here is a sampling:

- *Environmental health and safety officers* evaluate and coordinate the storage and handling of hazardous waste, and the sampling and cleanup of contaminated soil or water.

- *Ergonomists* analyze the design of industrial and office equipment to improve worker comfort, safety, and productivity.

- *Health physicists* help employees who work around radiation and/ or use radioactive materials. They protect workers from radiation exposure and from creating a hazard to the environment.

- *Industrial hygienists* survey and analyze the workplace for health hazards, including exposure to lead, asbestos, chemicals, pesticides, and communicable diseases, as well as poor air quality and excessive noise.

With environmental concerns increasing, OHSS roles are expanding to encompass ecological balance, and employee emotional- and mental-health issues associated with increased workloads and stress on the job.[103]

Most OHSS employers require trained specialists. Education can include a bachelor's degree in a science or engineering discipline, four-year degrees in safety and related subjects, or a master's degree (M.S. or M.P.H.).[104] Specialists interested in a research career may also pursue a doctoral degree aimed at solving the more fundamental problems in this field.

Related instructional programs include:

- Environmental Health and Safety

- Industrial Safety Technology

- Occupational Health and Industrial Hygiene

- Occupational Safety and Health Technology

- Quality Control and Safety Technologies[105]

According to the Bureau of Labor Statistics, occupational health and safety specialists held about 55,800 jobs in 2008. Projected growth is 11 percent, or sixty-two thousand jobs, in 2018. Employment growth is expected to continue due to public demand for a safe and healthy work environment. The majority of jobs found were spread throughout the private sector, while 41 percent of OHSS worked for federal, state, and local government agencies.[106]

The occupational health and safety field is constantly evolving and presents unique challenges and exciting opportunities in technology, national/international workforce demographics, and environmental regulations. The specialists are needed wherever the potential for human and ecological health hazards arise.[107]

Ellen's Story

Six years ago, Ellen Ray knew she was getting older and wanted to enhance her skills on the job. Ray, who has worked for the Orange County Sanitation District for the last twenty-five years, first began her career as a mechanic. She was the first woman mechanic hired at the company. Eventually, she became a certified crane-and-equipment operator and then, at the request of her safety manager, earned a certificate to train other employees on operating small cranes. She liked the training so much that she pursued her safety-training career in 2006 through a specialized OSHA-certificate program in Occupational Safety and Health.

The program is designed for those who want to learn the basics of safety. Instructors (all safety professionals) cover a wide variety of real-world safety and emergency-preparedness topics, including accident investigation, evacuation and emergency planning, fall prevention, machine-guarding, electrical procedures, working in confined spaces, public warehousing, business-disaster preparedness, and safety for small businesses.

"Until I went through the OSHA program, I didn't realize there was so much more for me to learn and know," confesses Ray, now safety and health representative for the Orange County Sanitation District in California. "The instructors are incredible. These men and women have a wealth of knowledge and have been in the field. I also really liked the classroom environment because you had people from all over the United States, from all types of trades. Now I have lifelong contacts and we still keep in touch. One of my contacts needed some fall-protection information so I helped him with that."

One of the courses Ray learned the most from focused on inspections.

"We did hazard inspections to get used to what to look for as far as making the work environment safer for staff, accident investigating, and how to go to a site and look at the whole picture and document it," she recalls. "I had never done any of this before. In my job, we deal with a lot of confined spaces. Since I have gone through more safety training, I feel good when I'm training our staff because I have been there. We have to always make sure people have the appropriate training, equipment, and written procedures before they start any job."

Ergonomics, Ray notes, is another important aspect of health and safety for any job. "Not only is ergonomics important for an aging workforce, but we also want to make sure the right tools are set up in the workplace to make it easier for people to do their jobs."

Ray is part of a growing number of professionals in various fields who are seeking more safety training. According to the U.S. Bureau of Labor Statistics, employment of occupational health and safety specialists and technicians is expected to increase 9 percent between 2006 and 2016. Emergency preparedness will continue to increase in importance, creating demand for these workers. More specialists will be needed to cope with future threats, technological advances in safety equipment, changing regulations, and increasing public expectations.

Ray, who starts her workday at 6:00 a.m. overseeing construction projects for the Orange County Sanitation District, notes that while there is a lot of training and education available for health-and-safety professionals, there is still a lot to learn.

"Things are changing all the time. Even with all the training on any given day, somebody will have fallen off a ladder or be injured in a trench," she admits. "As far as I'm concerned, even one person getting injured is one too many. We really try to push safety. I want people, when they come to work, to know that they are trained, and feel comfortable enough to do their job. I want them to know that I have done everything I can to mitigate any hazards. At the end of the day, they can go home to their families in one piece. I do feel like I make a difference."

9. Spanish/English Translation and Interpretation

Spanish is the official language in twenty-one countries. It is one of the fastest-spreading languages in the world, with more than 350 million Spanish-speakers worldwide, including 31 million in the United States.[108] It is estimated that by the year 2050, there will be more than 500 million Spanish-speakers, of which 100 million will be living in the U.S.[109]

The Hispanic population has recently become the largest minority in the United States. They are a major consumer group for Hispanic culture, products, and services.

This trend offers tremendous business opportunities in the Spanish-translation industry. Translation services are needed in a wide spectrum of industries, including: advertising, aerospace, automotive, business, chemical, contracts, defense, education, entertainment, energy, financial, government, immigration, globalization, law, manufacturing, marketing, media, medical, patents, religion, retail, software, technical, and telecommunications fields.[110]

There is an art to interpretation and translation that goes beyond simply translating the meaning of the words; Spanish/English language specialists convey concepts and ideas between the languages. Translators must have experience and knowledge of the subject matter in order to accurately express the meaning and values from one language and culture into another.[111]

Some Spanish/English language specialists do both interpretation and translation; however, they are two different professions. Specifically, interpreters specialize in the spoken word, while translators deal with written words. Each profession requires a specific and distinct set of skills and abilities.[112]

There are two modes of interpreting: simultaneous and consecutive. Simultaneous interpreting is unique and complex, and requires interpreters to listen and speak at the same time the speaker is talking. Consecutive interpreting begins only after the speaker has finished a group of words or sentences.[113] Translators specialize in accurately converting written materials from one language into another. They must have excellent writing, organizational, and analytical skills. They must pay close attention to the coherence, style, and tone of the written material so that the translation reads as though it came from the original document.[114]

Spanish translators are experiencing many job opportunities due to the growing Hispanic population in the United States. Of the nearly 5.5 million who speak Spanish in California, it is estimated that 650,000 speak very limited English.[115]

In particular, demand is strong for interpreters and translators in the health-care and legal fields, due to the critical nature of the information.[116] In California, the outlook for Spanish/English translators and interpreters is particularly rosy due to the immigrant population and close proximity to Mexico. Especially in the San Diego region, which borders Mexico, translation and interpretation services are in high demand. Growth in employment within this field is projected to increase in the United States by 22 percent between 2008 and 2018.[117]

Humphrey's Story

At the tender age of fifty-three, Humphrey Rincon is looking to change careers, and it may prove to be easier than he ever thought possible. "I've been a general contractor for twenty years," says Rincon. In 2005 he formed his own company, Habitable Creations, primarily doing residential remodels and turnkey projects. "But in 2008 the industry was really hurting, work became scarce, and I began to worry that I wouldn't be able to make ends meet." Rincon has a house, a wife, two grown children, and three others still living at home. "I had to find a new career and still continue to pay the bills. Scary stuff!" admits Rincon.

Born in Los Angeles to immigrant parents from South America, Rincon learned basic Spanish from his mother before he even started school. Later, he attended a medical school in Columbia, South America. Unfortunately, his health failed and after three years he was forced to drop out of the med school and return to the States, where he earned a bachelor of science in Health Care Administration from Cal State University Northridge in 1985.

After graduation, Rincon caught the construction bug while building his own home. He attended Pasadena City College for building and construction technology, and later got his general-contractor's license. For twenty years life was good for Rincon until the economy took a tumble and he was forced to look in new directions.

"Because of my bilingual background," says Rincon, "I initially began looking at court-interpreter programs." Rincon began pursuing a Translation and Interpretation Certificate program in 2008 at a university. Rincon is still working toward his certificate. "I'm about halfway through the course work, and I look forward to finishing, but I've had to drop classes a few times to make ends meet." Yet, even without the certificate, Rincon has witnessed a huge shift in his options. "The program teaches a more systematic approach and opens up resources," he adds. "I found out about Web sites and jobs that I didn't even know existed."

One of those jobs was for an FBI linguist position. Rincon scored well on the first and second tests, but didn't score high enough to be a linguist. The Washington office, however, still requested he continue and take the third exam, which is virtually unheard of, according to Rincon. "They said I did extremely well," he beams. "I scored a four-plus on English and a three-plus on Spanish, with five being the maximum and almost unobtainable, according to my contact at the FBI." Rincon said that his scores qualify him for a monitor position, and the FBI has now begun its arduous background check.

Through the program, Rincon also learned about the American Translators Association (ATA), a professional organization that offers a certification. "Even though I don't have the money right now to sit for the certification exam," says Rincon, "simply creating a profile and being a member has resulted in several e-mail and phone-call inquiries."

One of those was a connection to Morgan Language Services out of Maryland. "They perked up when I said I was in a continuing-education program. Shortly after that, I received a letter of intent basically telling me to name my own salary!"

Rincon also tested for and is awaiting the results of a language-interpreter position with the San Diego School District. He is really hoping the FBI position comes through, however. "I'd love to work for the federal government," he reveals. "I'm just thankful and blessed that I've found something that allows me to shift gears so radically. I found skills I didn't even know I had!"

While attending classes in Colombia, Rincon performed what he would later discover to be a specialized skill: sight translation (or the ability to read text in one language and speak it in another).

"Basically," recalls Rincon, "I bought my textbooks from L.A., where they often were a few editions ahead of those available in Columbia. My fellow students would ask what my book said because they knew it was more current. I did sight translation for them, not even knowing it was a specialized skill. I understand now that this is one of the more difficult things to become proficient in."

"We often underestimate our potential," concludes Rincon. "If you just start exploring avenues, check things out, and always be willing to listen, you never know what you'll discover."

10. Sustainable Business Practices and the Greening of All Jobs

By the mid-twenty-first century, all jobs will be green jobs. "Almost every single profession is turning green these days," says Vicki Krantz, UC San Diego Extension's director of business and professional programs. "If you're in accounting, you learn about carbon accounting. If you're in purchasing, you emphasize your ability to buy smarter and work with a 'green supply chain.' If you're in marketing, you focus on responding to the public demand for green."[118]

Green-collar jobs can be found in every profession. For example, green engineers are needed in the sustainable-energy and automotive industries. Accountants are needed to help businesses measure the extent of problems and solutions through analysis of company reports.[119]

Architects, urban planners, designers, and construction firms can align themselves with Leadership in Energy and Environmental Design (LEED).

LEED is an internationally recognized green-building-certification system that verifies that a building or community was designed and built to improve a variety of processes, including energy savings, water efficiency, CO2-emissions reduction, and improved indoor environmental quality.[120]

Going green will impact every job in every sector. Smart companies are encouraging a bottoms-up emphasis on green and sustainable practices. Many have infused a green awareness into day-to-day activities, such as turning off computer monitors or recycling paper. Big and small firms are incorporating green initiatives examining how their business affects the environment.[121]

Some of the biggest employers have ongoing green initiatives. Bank of America has reduced its paper use by 32 percent and recycles thirty thousand tons of paper each year. Hewlett-Packard and Dell have adopted e-waste recycling programs that shred obsolete computer products, so the raw materials can be recycled. Starbucks uses coffee-cup sleeves made of recycled paper, saving roughly seventy-eight thousand trees per year since 2006. Walmart has launched a long-term plan to power all its stores with 100-percent¬–renewable-energy sources.[122]

According to green entrepreneur Tom Szaky,[123] sustainability should be an integral part of an employee's day-to-day responsibilities. All employers, both large and small, should rethink their way of doing business and become more socially responsible about the environment, he believes. Every employee can make a difference by adjusting energy settings for heating and cooling systems, turning off computer monitors when not in use, carpooling to work, purchasing recycled paper and green products, and practicing sustainability to reduce a company's carbon footprint.[124]

In fact, companies are learning that sustainable business practices not only help the environment, but also can improve profitability and efficiency, reduce waste and liability, and contribute to better community relations.[125]

Sustainability practices save money and reduce environmental impact. Both large and small employers can set green policies and make changes to everyday business practices, and all employees would share in this responsibility. In effect, being fluent in the language of green is rapidly becoming an important part of every professional's vocabulary.[126]

Leslie's Story

Every now and then a positive story comes out of a bad economy. Leslie Widner's story is one of those. Widner, a Bay Area native, moved to San Diego to attend San Diego State University. She received her bachelor of arts degree in 2007 and a Multiple-Subject Teaching Credential in 2008. An internship teaching second- and third-graders prepared Widner for her goal after graduation: to secure a grade-school teaching job.

Unfortunately for Widner and many other hopeful educators during the recession, teaching jobs were few and far between in 2008. Frustrated and desperate, Widner took a job at a large hotel chain as a front-office supervisor. Once there, she reignited her second passion: caring for the environment.

"I saw such an enormous amount of waste there," says Widner. "They had no recycling at all and probably used a ream of paper a day." She set up a recycling program at the hotel and soon began researching school curriculums locally for a program that would expand her expertise in this area.

While reading an article about green events in San Diego, Widner came across a Sustainable Business Practices Certificate program.

"Sustainability," explains Widner, "is understanding how a business affects the environment and the people in the community." Outsourcing to other countries is also a part of the equation. Sustainability looks at how those countries conduct business. How do they affect the environment? A company can't boast minimal environmental impact if they're outsourcing their products or work to a country that does business without the environment in mind. "It's about the three 'E's,'" adds Widner. "Environment, Education and Equity, and, of course, creating a minimal amount of waste."

The Certificate program offered classes like integrating sustainability into business practices, environmental economics, and green marketing and positioning. It was exactly what she needed: She could attend at her own pace, the course work was what she wanted, and it was priced right for her budget.

Widner was intimidated by her first experience in class. "Initially I felt I was in the wrong program. It seemed like the classes were geared toward the business person," she admits. "I had to do a lot of catching up just in the terminology used; I didn't even know what ROI [return on investment] meant!"

But Widner notes that her professors were knowledgeable, kind, and encouraging. They persuaded her to share her experiences in class and to stick with it. Fortuitously, an internship facilitated by the program also helped land Widner a job as soon as she obtained her Certificate.

"We had a speaker on the first day of class, Gary Goodson, the executive director of U.S. Green Building Council, San Diego," recalls Widner. USGBC is a national nonprofit dedicated to creating sustainable living. "I really liked what he had to say, so I e-mailed him about volunteer opportunities. Two weeks later, I had an internship!" That internship, and Widner's newly obtained Sustainable Business Practices Certificate, opened the door to her current job with Waste Less Living, Inc.

Waste Less Living, based in Pasadena, provides composting services and education to schools, special events, and businesses. As a sales consultant, Widner now combines both of her passions: teaching and acting as a steward of the environment. One of Widner's responsibilities is to go into school lunchrooms and show children how they can have minimal impact on the environment.

"It's awesome to see the change in the kids' thinking after we spend some time together and I show them a few simple things they can do to make a change!" exclaims Widner. "Our first pilot school converted to a 76-percent diversion rate—meaning 76 percent of their waste now goes to a composting facility. The kids get immense joy and pride in seeing how they can help."

The Certificate program also gives Widner credibility in her job. "It's exciting to be in a conversation with my boss and be able to contribute thoughtful information based on my classroom experiences in the certificate program," she reports. "She's impressed by my knowledge, and I surprise myself because with most of the topics that come up, I'm able to discuss and contribute helpful information!"

With her newfound direction in life, Widner offers perceptive advice to others thinking about or, perhaps, being forced to make a career change.

"Look at your life and look at the consistencies in it. Find something you're already passionate about, research a program that will enhance your knowledge, go for it, and don't even worry about the economy."

11. Teaching Adult Learners

Adult education is one of the few industries that has seen positive growth throughout a tough economy. Job-seekers unable to find employment in their desired fields are going back to school to further their education in other industries. According to the U.S. Bureau of Labor Statistics in 2009, private education was one of only two industries that posted job growth.[127]

An increasing number of postsecondary educators are also providing career-related education to working adults. Instructors are needed to provide these types of programs, which offer flexible work schedules. Many classes are offered on nights and weekends, or online, in order to accommodate older students and those who work or have family obligations. In most cases, only a few instructor hours are required during the week for student lectures, consultations, and administrative responsibilities. It is expected that postsecondary teaching positions will increase 15 percent by 2018.[128]

Frequently, adult learners take courses for pleasure or self-improvement. As a large number of the population retires and has more time for taking courses, the need for self-enrichment teachers is expected to increase. Self-enrichment educators are expected to increase 32 percent by 2018.[129]

The leading self-enrichment courses encompass life skills, recreation, academic subjects, computer software and hardware, and foreign languages. Students have an increasing demand for topics on self-improvement, personal finance, computers, and Internet-related subjects.[130]

The main qualification for employment in this industry is being an expert in the subject area. Formal training may be required for some areas such as art or music. Employment opportunities for self-enrichment-education instructors are expected to grow faster than most occupations. Job opportunities appear more often due to the short-term nature of the courses.

Often adult educators can advance from part-time to full-time positions or move into coordinator or administrative positions. Self-enrichment teachers can advance into a supervisory role or start their own programs or schools.

12. Teaching English as a Foreign Language

In the last few years, demand for overseas English-language teaching positions has spiked. College graduates find lucrative teaching positions abroad in almost any country in Europe, Asia, Africa, Central America, and South America. Teaching abroad is a great opportunity for those who desire to work and travel, as opposed to teaching in a U.S. public-school setting.[131]

Students worldwide are eager to learn English, because the language is and will remain the language of international business for the immediate future. The demand for English as a foreign language (EFL) and English as a second language (ESL) is strong, both domestically and abroad. English teachers are also needed in specialized fields, such as engineering, aviation, and medicine.

Domestically, opportunities for ESL teachers are highest in states such as California, Texas, New York, and Florida. With high immigration rates in these states, a significant portion of the population has limited abilities to read, write, and speak English.

However, many of non-native limited-English-speaking immigrants have also begun settling in Midwestern cities, thereby increasing the demand for ESL teachers in the heartland. As limited-English speakers move to different areas of the country to pursue economic opportunities, the demand for ESL teachers travels with them.

The soft economy also pushes demand for ESL training. Employers tend to increase employment standards in a weak market. Thus, more job-seekers enroll in ESL programs to gain a competitive edge.[132] Varying levels of expertise and credentials are required to teach ESL, depending upon the class type and students' language abilities. Entry-level ESL teachers need to have a bachelor's degree, as well as certification in Teaching English to Speakers of Other Languages (TESOL) and a state-level teaching certification. ESL teachers aiming for jobs in higher education at community colleges and universities must have a master's degree.

Teaching overseas requires a TESOL certificate and a work visa. Presently, many TESOL-certification training courses can be completed in just a few weeks. ESL and TEFL teachers have ample opportunities for traveling and teaching abroad. Teachers with prior knowledge of the language and culture of their prospective students generally have the advantage.[133] However, some programs do hire those teachers who lack knowledge of the native culture and language, but who have a talent for creative communication skills. Despite modest salaries, living and working in a foreign country can make this an attractive career choice.[134]

13. Marine Biodiversity and Conservation

Changes in temperature, sea level, and ocean chemistry have enormous implications for marine biodiversity and ecosystem functions.[135] Maintaining the integrity of ocean ecosystems and managing their use in this rapidly changing global environment is one of the greatest challenges of this century.

Overfishing and destructive fishing techniques worldwide wipe out marine mammals and entire ecosystems. The rate of depletion of the world's fisheries has increased more than four times in the past forty years. However, proper management of marine resources and habitat conservation can revitalize a depleted marine ecosystem.

Marine scientists have the opportunity to protect the reefs on a large scale by declaring fishing off-limits. Management of declared areas and total closures, which protect against fishing and pollution, allow fish stocks and coral-reef fisheries to recover dramatically. Traditional management strategies have resulted in 300 percent more fish and almost double the size of healthy corals in such areas as Papua New Guinea and Indonesia.[136] More investments in conservation projects like these provide more job opportunities for conservation scientists, marine ecologists, fisheries scientists, and policymakers for the oceans.

Policymakers are taking action to protect high-seas biodiversity. Andrew Rosenberg, a fisheries scientist at the University of New Hampshire, says, "In many cases it is not the science that is at issue, but the political reality of making changes in the way we have used and abused natural resources."[137] If a development project is happening in the vicinity of a sensitive marine habitat, scientists need to monitor before, during, and after construction to ensure that proper techniques and actions are followed.

Opportunities are expected to grow for marine-science professionals, science-policy analysts, advocates, and natural scientists. Jobs are also expected to open for those interested in becoming involved in public policy and economics of marine conservation.

Cali Turner Tomaszewicz, a MAS MBC graduate who works for WSSI, an environmental consulting firm in San Diego, California, states, "I believe that despite the challenges facing our oceans today, there are many things we can do to make a difference that impacts both the condition of our oceans, and our own communities that rely on coastal and ocean resources."[138]

14. Health Law

Legal and medical experts agree that health law is one of the fastest-growing areas of legal practice. Medical decisions have become extremely complex and practitioners are looking for ways to influence policy regarding health care. Health-care reform is just one of several reasons for growth in this sector. Additional reasons include more government regulation of health care, the rise of bioethical and biotechnology issues, tort reform related to malpractice, aging of the baby boomer generation, and the consequent growth of Medicare.

The specialization of Health Law is a master's degree, abbreviated LL.M., awarded to lawyers after receiving their law degree. LL.M. Health Law programs usually require an additional year of study. Integration of medical-legal issues spans a wide range of career interests, such as health-care administration, program and policy development, public health, biomedical and biotechnical research, and the pharmaceutical industry.

Primary settings for practicing health-care law are nonprofit advocacy and public-interest organizations, hospitals, health services corporations, health administration and regulatory government agencies, and public-interest firms. For example, one nonprofit advocacy organization is the National Health Law Project (NHLP), which works to improve health care for the impoverished, uninsured, unemployed, minorities, elderly, and disabled. Nonprofit corporations are mostly comprised of hospitals and community clinics.[139]

Government agencies at both the state and federal levels need Health Law professionals to develop program policies and to promulgate regulations. The U.S. Department of Health and Human Services (HHS) is the leading federal agency that formulates health-care policy and regulations. HHS employs hundreds of lawyers in a wide range of agencies, such as the Food and Drug Administration and Medicare.

In recent years, federal and state legislators have focused on public health-care policy. As a result, health-care providers, pharmaceutical companies, health-insurance companies, and private public-interest firms need Health Law professionals to advocate on their behalf.

The Bureau of Labor Statistics projects fairly strong job growth in coming years for postsecondary teachers and researchers of all kinds.[140] Law-school graduates who wish to take the academic route can become Health Law professors, teachers, and researchers.

Tim's Story

When Tim Mackey began studying for a master's degree in a newly minted Health Law program in San Diego, he wanted to better understand the compliance and legal issues in play at the medical-device company where he works. But his studies led to the opportunity to coauthor treatises that have opened doors academically and professionally, resulting in a promotion and the inspiration to take a long look at the university's doctorate program. "It changed my life," Mackey proclaims. "Without exaggeration, my experience in the program has already given me opportunities I'd never dreamed of."

Mackey is one of the first to earn a master's degree in Health Law from the UC San Diego School of Medicine and California School of Law, which jointly launched the program in 2008 to begin shining better light on the issues that fall where health-care issues and legal issues intersect. Most people in the program come from either a health-care or legal background and need to learn more about the other set of principles, issues, and challenges with which they are not familiar.

At 30, Mackey had already earned a bachelor's degree in political science, with a focus on international relations. He worked as a paralegal and eventually was hired by a medical-device company, where he works on compliance and legal issues.

"When I read about the program, which informs you about both health care and legal issues, I thought it might help me better understand the challenges that my company faces," Mackey said. "I wanted to hone my skill set to a particular industry and I had no idea that I would get to study with such amazing people." Mackey studied for a year and a half, graduating in June 2009. "It's a flexible program; I did an accelerated course, but it's supposed to take two years," he reveals to us. "It's geared toward working professionals who bring real-world experience to the classroom."

According to the prospectus, the eight-course, graduate-level curriculum is designed to orient professionals to the common activities, philosophy of practice, and challenges of the companion discipline in health care or law. The program focuses on acculturating practitioners in both fields to become leaders in providing integrated, sensitive solutions to everyday practice and policy issues.

Mackey said there were about twenty students in his cohort, which meant that they worked closely with instructors. "I was the youngest person in the program. I was surrounded by doctors, scientists, and legal specialists, so I got to interact with physicians, clinicians, lawyers, compliance officers—a whole cross-section of people with a tremendous amount of professional experience and knowledge."

Brian Liang, who has both an M.D. and a J.D. and teaches both medicine and law at the two different schools, worked closely with the small group of students in the program. "Professor Liang put in a lot of extra effort to further my education; he really made the program powerful and accessible to a wide range of students," Mackey recalls. "He was kind enough to mentor me and give me the opportunity to coauthor articles. I would have never had a chance to do this without him and the program."

At work, Mackey was promoted to a better paying and more interesting position. "There's so much regulation in the medical-device industry that the acquired skill set is vital, whether you are an attorney or you're writing the packet instructions," he explains. "I came away from the program with practice in solving problems and looking at questions that have both medical and legal issues."

Mackey is now looking at Ph.D. programs and may well pursue one—something he hadn't considered before he began his studies. "The program has changed my life," he says. "It provided me with a very specific skill set in a growing industry, and it made me immediately more valuable, as well as giving me some great new long-term goals and plans."

15. Welding

Nearly 100 percent of welding-school graduates are finding rapid job placement, according to Ray Shook, executive director of the American Welding Society (AWS).[141] Employers don't have a shortage of applicants; they have a shortage of qualified applicants with technical skills. While about 500,000 welders are currently working in the U.S, the average welder is now nearing retirement age, with twice as many welders retiring as being trained. As of 2010, the AWS estimates the U.S. will be short of more than 200,000 welders.

Major industries that employ welders include aircraft manufacturing, shipbuilding, commercial construction, and transportation. About 65 percent of welding jobs are found in manufacturing. Jobs are concentrated in fabricated-metal-product manufacturing, transportation-equipment manufacturing, and machinery manufacturing, as well as architectural- and structural-metals manufacturing and construction.

Stimulus projects created under the American Recovery and Reinvestment Act have raised the demand for skilled blue-collar workers even more. Thousands of infrastructure projects such as repair of roads and bridges, mass transit and railways, and green retrofitting require skilled welders to get the job done. Welding jobs can also be found in "green" industries, including wind-energy systems, solar-energy installations, and retrofitting of buildings for energy efficiency.

Abundant career opportunities can also be found in automation, an important emerging technology. The U.S. has hundreds of thousands of arc-welding robots, which need to be programmed by robotic-arc-welding technicians.[142] Although automation can handle basic welding tasks, the more detailed welding tasks required by many manufacturing and construction operations still can only be done by highly-skilled welders.

Rapid development of advanced materials creates a demand for welding pros. Reliable joining methods are needed for materials such as super alloys, composites, and modern ceramics.[143]

The shortage of skilled welders makes recruitment a priority for some trade groups like the AWS. The National Association of Manufacturers, an industry group located in Washington, D.C., started programs that give students and young adults hands-on interaction and positive images of modern welding as an attractive career path.[144]

Welding certification validates that a specific level of skill and training has been achieved. Most employers require candidates to pass a welder qualification test as a prerequisite for employment. Some employers have developed their own internal certification tests.145 Another avenue for attaining certification is to complete a short welding program offered at a community college or private technical school. The AWS offers a certification program where the credential is transferrable. Their courses have been incorporated in many welding certification programs across the country. A welding-school locator tool can be found on the AWS Web site.[146]

According to the Bureau of Labor Statistics, welders can advance to more skilled welding jobs with additional training and experience. Career prospects for welders who have advanced on-the-job experience include: welding technicians, supervisors, inspectors, and instructors. Some experienced welders open their own repair shops. Others, especially those with a bachelor's degree or many years of experience, may become welding engineers.[147]

Ernest's Story

Ernest Levert, a former president of AWS, is a senior-staff manufacturing engineer at Lockheed Martin Missiles and Fire Control in Dallas, Texas. As a welding engineer, Levert has taken on tough assignments such as using an electron-beam welding process to fuse live missiles.

The Lockheed Martin Missiles and Fire Control company is one of six companies that comprise Lockheed Martin Electronic Systems.

The company develops, manufactures, and supports advanced combat, missile, rocket, and space systems for military customers that include the U.S. Army, Navy, Air Force, and Marine Corps, as well as NASA and dozens of foreign nations. The company also offers products and services for the global civil nuclear-power industry. All in all, the company does business in more than fifty countries and offers more than forty product lines.

Now Levert is working on thermal control panels for the International Space Station. He graduated from a vocational-high-school welding program and then from the U.S. Navy's C-1 Welding School.

During his junior year at Ohio State University, Levert met U.S. astronaut Ron McNair, whose advice he always remembered. "He told me to take an area of my discipline and become a specialist. Don't just become a typical mediocre welding engineer. Pick an area and become an expert."[148]

16. Action Sports

Job-seekers searching for a strong sector should consider this: Despite the current economic slump, the surf/skate industry has shown notable resiliency during recent global economic challenges, posting U.S. retail sales of $7.22 billion in 2008, according to the Surf Industry Manufacturers Association (SIMA). Although that was down slightly from 2006 ($7.48 billion), the surf industry has shown substantial growth of 10 percent for the past five years, according to SIMA.

There are several associations and trade groups across the nation that support and help fuel the growing sporting-goods market, including the Sporting Goods Manufacturing Association. CONNECT, a San

Diego-based nonprofit innovation-business accelerator, is doing its part to stimulate the already strong action-sports industry in Southern California through a new program called CONNECT Sports & Entertainment Innovators, headed by former NBA star Bill Walton.

Walton is leading local efforts to strengthen and accelerate the growth of San Diego's start-up and growth-stage entertainment and sports-related companies for entrepreneurs through educational programs, business mentoring, and access to capital. The program will connect entrepreneurs with the local research community, advanced materials, and solutions to making entertainment and sports products more competitive, greener, and safer. The business accelerator also facilitates licensing, merger and acquisition, and strategic partnership opportunities for innovation-stage companies by connecting them with major industry players.

Walton claims San Diego is a perfect venue to support the sports-and-entertainment industry, which includes everything from surf and skateboard apparel and products to sports teams and companies that cater to professional and amateur athletes. The region, which even has its own Olympic Training Center, is home to a plethora of professional athletes, including surfers, skateboarders, wakeboarders, triathletes, soccer players, football players, and motocross stars.

According to CONNECT, sports enterprises are among the largest business clusters in the San Diego region, with more than six hundred sports-related companies.

Of course, Southern California is synonymous with fitness. As a result, job-seekers who are interested in a possible career in the multibillion-dollar sporting-goods market in this region will have plenty of options. In particular, the state is a mecca for the action-sports industry, including surfing, skateboarding, and snowboarding. Top retail companies such as Volcom, Quicksilver, O'Neill, No Fear, Sector 9, and Body Glove all have So Cal headquarters.

Southern California is also home to professional skateboarder Tony Hawk; pro surfers such as Rob Machado, Tim Curran, Pat O'Connell, Joel Tudor, Dane Reynolds, and Chris Ward; and professional snowboarder Shaun White, who took home the Olympic gold medal in 2010. Some of the world's legendary surf spots are located in Southern California as well, including Trestles, Malibu, and Huntington Beach. Some of the world's biggest extreme-sports events including the X Games, Boost Mobile Pro, and U.S. Open of Surfing are all in Southern California

Meanwhile, the annual Transpacific Yacht Race from Los Angeles to Hawaii is one of yachting's premier events. The San Diego Yacht Club held the America's Cup—the most prestigious prize in yachting—from 1988 to 1995, and hosted three America's Cup races during that time.

Job-seekers in the sports industry also have the option of working for the many sports franchises and sports networks, such as Fox Sports and ESPN, both of which have affiliates in Southern California.

JOB SEEKERS, LISTEN TO THE VOICE OF THE EMPLOYER

When you read an ad looking for an employee with a certain level of experience and skills, do you ever wonder what the employer wants? In the current economic situation, where it seems that employers can have anyone they want at almost any salary, what do they really want?

> **"What were employers looking for? There were three key factors that would enable the prospective employee to be hired and would predict the success of the employee."**

Over the past twelve years, significant research has been conducted on employer preferences, also known as the "Voice of the Employer" studies. Researchers have been intrigued by who gets hired and who does not as we have gone through the economic crisis of 9/11, the boom in the years afterward, and the current economic downturn. When the Workforce Investment Act was passed by Congress in 1998, federal money became available for job-seekers to get trained for new careers, and for employers to hire the workers, once trained. A number of studies have been conducted in the intervening years to find out what employers wanted in a job applicant. The research has continued to this day, with little change in their description of what kind of worker they would hire.

In the studies, employers of all types were interviewed and surveyed about all kinds of jobs, from entry-level workers with limited experience in the field in which they were applying to experts who were well seasoned. Typically, the employers were interviewed individually. Groups of employers organized the data obtained from all of the interviews into key attributes and rated the importance of each attribute. Throughout all of that economic turmoil, what employers seek in employees has not changed much.

What are employers looking for? There are three key factors that would enable the prospective employee to be hired and would predict the success of the employee. The employers are looking for evidence of these three key factors in each prospect. Surprisingly, many job-seekers were unable to produce direct evidence of these three factors.

Factor #1: Employers want proof that a prospect has the necessary knowledge, training, and experience to perform the job or, at least, to learn how to perform it. Preferably, the prospect has both. What is important is not only the training and experience, but the demonstrated ability to learn! The employer examines the resumé, attitude, and approach of the prospects.

Of greater importance to the employer is certification of the ability to do the job, or certification of the knowledge and skills that will allow the prospect to learn how to do the job. A track record of success in similar jobs is preferred, but the key is to be able to point to evidence—proof—of abilities to perform and learn. At the time of the study, the interviewed employers perceived that the nimbleness of their organization and the rapidly changing marketplace required them to have employees who could adapt and change with the marketplace. Direct experience, while relevant, wasn't then—and still isn't—as important as the demonstrated ability to adapt and perform in new circumstances.

Many people are changing careers in the current job climate. Engineers are becoming marketers. Production employees are going back to school to develop new skills. In many fields, when changing jobs or careers, certifications are available and can be obtained with the proper training. The candidate who has certified skills and evidence of the ability to learn, even at an advanced stage of his or her career, is essential. Someone who is experienced and able to learn is thought to be more versatile than another, younger candidate—more adaptable to changing circumstances. In this economy, that is the kind of ability that companies want to hire!

A survey of business leaders within the past six months has indicated that candidates with a track record of finding ways to cut costs are also highly desirable. Even while others were laid off, employers hired people who knew how to cut costs in production, marketing, or services. Evidence of this type of background or training by prospects, while difficult to obtain, may be of great benefit to employers at any time—good economy or bad.

Factor #2: The employers want evidence that the prospective employee will be dependable at work—that they will be available for work every day. Surprisingly, few prospects record or mention their attendance record at school, at work, or in the training/certification program they have just completed. Very few agencies, references, or instructors mention attendance as an important aspect of their training either. The employers assume that if the prospect did not have great attendance when being trained for their new career or in their old job, there may be trouble in the future. How dependable would they be at work? There are instances when a prospect is selected after a lengthy interviewing process, but then the employee exhibits a minor attendance problem during the company orientation. Despite the time and energy invested in finding the employee, many companies perceive even minor attendance issues as early indicators of future problems and fire the lackadaisical new hire. They will not spend any more time, effort, or money on someone who is too casual about showing up for work.

Illness and other concerns can cause attendance issues. Employers want to know that the work they have assigned will be taken care of and the strategies they have attempted to implement will not suffer. Employers know and understand the costs of poor attendance, both direct (lost labor, lost production) and indirect (effects on other staff of picking up the load). The frequency and costs associated with casual absences— those not caused directly by illness—have been on the rise since the mid-1990s. This has caused stress and morale problems at work that have led to more absences.[149] Employers want to combat this trend by hiring prospects with great attendance records.

Factor #3: Similarly, the employers want to know that the prospect will come to work and meetings on time. In the studies, punctuality was another key element of evaluation. The employers believe that attendance is not good enough on its own; the prospect has to have a track record of being on time. Habitual lateness, even just for meetings, is viewed as disrespectful. Many meetings are now virtual meetings, with remote attendees. The need to be on time becomes more critical with virtual meetings. Tying up several employees waiting for another becomes increasingly expensive and decreases workflow productivity. Employers desire evidence of not only attendance, but of punctuality as well.

As research has indicated, poor punctuality may be a reflection of what we expect others to do.[150] If others are likely to be late, then being a few minutes late may not cost us any waiting time, but the employer may think about what it costs the business. Employers in the U.S. expect their employees to be on time, despite what other cultures and traditions may dictate.[151] Chronic lateness has been shown to cost employers billions of dollars.[152] Entire countries have attempted to answer employers' desires for better punctuality by conducting national crusades against lateness.

Employers have many options in the current marketplace for recruiting employees. They can hire someone from within. They can hire no one and contract the work on the outside. Hiring a prospect is a big investment for most companies, even more so for smaller companies. The ability to do the job, as well as to learn and adapt to the job, are viewed as necessary, but not sufficient. Employers want workers who show up on time each day for every single meeting or assignment.

FINAL THOUGHTS

The authors hope the ideas and concepts introduced in Section One will prove useful to understanding the opportunities and challenges ahead, as well as some ways of successfully navigating the ever-changing requirements of an innovation economy and the rapidly changing requirements in the workplace. Section Two provides a case study of San Diego, a region that has done this reasonably well, and an examination of what these changing realities mean for policymakers and employers.

SECTION TWO

AN ECONOMY WITH GOOD JOBS FOR ALL

CHAPTER 5

You Don't Have to Live in Silicon Valley to be Successful in the Innovation Age

T he immediate challenge across the United States, as we have attempted to describe in the previous section, is this: How do we, as a nation, accelerate innovation while assuring that we have the skilled workforce we need to deploy and engage these new technologies, so that we will not have to import labor or export jobs? It has become abundantly clear that, even though the United States has done a superb job of leading global innovation through its research universities and institutes, its entrepreneurial spirit and commercialization capabilities, and its favorable fiscal environment for high-risk ventures, the beneficiaries of this process have been narrower than what is in America's long-term competitive interest. A report published by the Metropolitan Policy Center of the Brookings Institution in May 2010 dramatically documented this phenomenon. Their assessment of economic developments in one hundred metropolitan regions across the United States over the last decade yields a picture of overall decline in median wages and a growing gap between the top-10-percent earners in the population and the rest of the country. This income gap has been characterized as an emerging "hourglass economy" and has been a

> "America's competitiveness is equally dependent on the willingness of the American people to return to an economy based on investment and production, rather than borrowing and consumption."

concern of demographers and economists over the last two decades.[153]

The problem is so acute that President Obama tasked Vice President Joseph Biden with chairing a task force to examine how to restore America's middle class. This problem relates to America's declining competitiveness around the world. This decaying competitiveness is clearly, in part, a result of the growth in economic capacity in previously second- and third-world economies. These emerging economies are positioned to provide more than just cheaper manufacturing and services. Increasingly, they are a source of higher-quality manufacturing and services. They are also making significant contributions to invention and innovation, which provide the core technologies for new products that enable the growth of globally competitive companies. However, America's challenge today is also partially due to the relative complacency of the industry and workers who, after decades of global leadership, have been slow to recognize the shifting centers of economic gravity. The United States's competitiveness is based on the dynamic interplay of a variety of public and private investments, public policy vis-à-vis research, creative business practices, favorable trade policies and, of course, a skilled world-class workforce. But, America's competitiveness is equally dependent on the willingness of the American people to return to an economy based on investment and production, rather than borrowing and consumption. Continued prosperity is about values and culture, not just policy and investments. The question confronting all of us is: Are we ready to change not only public priorities but also our everyday habits?

San Diego is an instructive case when thinking about the challenges and opportunities that lie ahead and how to harness various forces that enable innovation, economic growth, job creation, and sustainable prosperity. The Brookings report of May 2010 put San Diego—a once sleepy, cul-de-sac city at the southernmost border of California— into the ranks of what they call diverse metro regions, which include iconic cities such as New York, Chicago, and San Francisco. The Brookings analysis pointed out that the median wage in San Diego during the decade's study went up 4.3 percent, while the median across the nation, as a whole, went down 4.1 percent. San Diego, in a period of three to four decades, has moved from an economy characterized by tourism, military contracting, and land and housing development, to one that is anchored by seven globally competitive technology-based clusters which have created not only new economic horizons, but a changing social and cultural landscape in a region previously ignored by most in the United States.

For this reason, San Diego represents an interesting case study. There is a tendency to look at superstar regions, such as Boston and the Silicon Valley, when attempting to unravel what enables innovation, wealth creation, and job creation on a scale that can be transformative for a region. The current scale of the innovation economy in these two regions, their distinctive industrial legacies, and their more than seventy-five years of building innovation economies represents a formidable challenge for sorting out how to replicate the outcomes they have achieved. Local conditions and industrial legacies are so different, and the need for transformation is so immediate in other parts of the country, that it is difficult to derive implementable lessons from Silicon Valley. San Diego, on the other hand, has accomplished an amazing transformation in half the time, with far fewer assets to begin with than either the Boston area or the San Francisco Bay area. As such, it is possible to deconstruct many of the economic, business, and social strategies that enabled its transformation. It is also possible to extract clues about how social and economic transformation occurs, and even principles of practice that are potentially relevant to other regions around the United States and the world. San Diego is an archetypical example of the power of collaboration in accelerating commercialization. The region is also archetypical for the significance of achieving alignment to assure that the regional workforce is ready for the new technologies and emerging companies that are likely to affect regional economic horizons.

Additionally, the very personal experiences of entrepreneurs and young college graduates who have migrated to the region over the last three decades represent stories of success with which individuals from other parts of the United States can identify and from which lessons can be drawn. It is the goal of this chapter to uncover some of these clues and suggest some of the principles of innovation coming out of the experience of San Diego's transformation.

HOW SAN DIEGO BUILT ITS RESEARCH AND DEVELOPMENT CAPACITY[154]

Before addressing the ways in which, thanks to innovation, the talent and workforce development systems have been linked to the creation of thousands of jobs and an increased median wage, it is important to share a little history. One of the book's authors, Mary Walshok, has been intimately involved in the transformation of the region, both as a dean and faculty member at UC San Diego and as a founder of CONNECT (1985), a nonprofit organization that is internationally recognized as a key catalyst for innovation and entrepreneurship in the region.

In the '50s and '60s, no one in America would have seen San Diego as a "center of excellence," a global player, or a "city on the move." It was a military hub in a fabulously beautiful location that attracted tourists, utopians, health nuts, and sports enthusiasts. In the 1950s, San Diego was not as economically, culturally, or intellectually dynamic as St. Louis, Pittsburgh, or Indianapolis—cities that presently look to San Diego as a model of economic transformation. However, things were happening in the region and in the state, at that time, which created a platform for forms of innovation and growth that no one could have anticipated. Forty years ago, regions such as Minneapolis, Philadelphia, and St. Louis already had:

- World class research universities and research centers

- Capital in the form of corporate, foundation, and personal wealth

- Affordable land

- Business-friendly taxes and public policies

Based on these assets, they should have developed into high-tech "new economy" hubs. However, they have yet to build the kinds of new economy clusters that create high-wage jobs for citizens and new forms of wealth for the region.

In contrast, over this same time period, the San Diego region has nurtured several thriving new economy clusters: biotechnology, wireless communications, clean tech, software, and innovative sports, to complement its historically strong defense-contracting and tourism clusters. These new economy clusters are anchored by the intellectual creativity of UC San Diego and other world-class research centers such as The Scripps Research Institute (TSRI), Salk Institute for Biological Studies (Salk), and Sanford-Burnham Medical Research Institute. San Diego has been able to transform its economic base in response to new global imperatives, creating more than four thousand new tech companies in three decades. The city has created tens of thousands of new technology jobs, including more than 100,000 new high-wage jobs in the life-sciences and wireless sectors alone. Its median wage levels have been progressively increasing, so that today, it is comparable to New York, Chicago, and San Francisco. How has San Diego been able to do this?

At present, San Diego has the kind of thriving ecosystem essential to innovation and competitiveness described in the previous chapter, even though forty years ago it did not. Other than affordable land, it lacked all the other factors outlined above. There was no world-class research university or capital for starting ventures, and, until the 1980s, its regional economic-development policies did not embrace technology entrepreneurship as a way of growing jobs for the regional economy. What it did have was a collaborative community interested in innovation, a long history of entrepreneurial ventures (some of which succeeded, most of which failed), and a willingness to approach economic growth through science and technology. This was enabled by a group of fledgling research institutions founded in the '50s and '60s—General Dynamics, Salk, TSRI, and UC San Diego—on the principle of building excellence quickly through great science. San Diego benefited equally from commitment by the private sector to support the creation of research institutes and a new university. Its collaborative culture resulted in the creation and growth of a special place anchored initially by world-class research and R & D talent, followed by a rapid growth in technology entrepreneurs, capital, and globally significant companies. The San Diego case is a fascinating example of how a region can enable research and enterprise and develop the type of workforce needed to deploy and apply new technologies in new companies. This simultaneous development would not have been possible without the creation of a variety of intermediary and integrative institutional mechanisms to support commercialization, nurture start-ups, and reskill the regional workforce.

To understand the economic transformation of San Diego over the last four decades, it is essential to understand five catalytic factors that were prerequisites to the rise of high-tech entrepreneurship in the San Diego region and, with that, the job growth and increase in average incomes. Each of these factors was necessary, but each alone was not sufficient. The five factors were:

- The role of regional-land-use decisions and state-infrastructure investments in the 1950s and 1960s.

- The focus, in the early 1960s, on building globally competitive basic-research institutions from the ground up.

- The long history of a local culture of collaboration between all the relevant parties (private, public, and academic), which goes beyond networking and involves shared agenda-setting, shared investment, shared risk, and shared rewards. This culture of collaboration includes a high tolerance for risk and failed ventures rooted in San Diego's volatile regional economy, which has experienced several severe boom/bust cycles since the late 1880s.

- A major commitment of time and resources by the private sector (mainly a collection of small and medium-sized enterprises, businesses, and professional services, as well as local philanthropy) to pool assets in order to support new and uncertain entrepreneurial ventures at pivotal points in the region's history.

- A powerful sense of place, which continues to bind people, if only for lifestyle, to the San Diego region and creates incentives for making things work, as well as helping new initiatives and enterprises to start and succeed through a reinvestment of personal time, connections, and cash.

1. Regional land use decisions. In the late 1940s, following the end of World War II, the San Diego economy, which had boomed during the war years, went into a severe post-war slump. Civic and business leaders, particularly in the defense-contracting industry led by John Jay Hopkins, CEO of Convair, concluded that the region's stability rested with a nuclear future, and, therefore, the region needed to attract physicists and engineers to a place that previously had not had a significant concentration of scientists. A privately funded think tank—General Atomics—was created, which quickly secured millions in federal research funding. This was followed by a bid to establish a new university campus, for which local businesses lobbied the state and city governments to create a school of engineering to train engineers for the local defense-contracting industry in a place that had never had a research university. Roger Revelle, then director of the Scripps Institution of Oceanography (SIO) urged the University of California Regents to found a new campus of the University of California that would be the equivalent of a public version of Caltech, using a decommissioned military base on the Torrey Pines Mesa, Camp Matthews, adjacent to SIO. To make this plan even more attractive, the local business community convinced the San Diego City Council to donate additional city lands on the Torrey Pines Mesa for this new university. General Atomics, still a division of General Dynamics, had already located a new research facility on city-contributed acreage nearby, on the Torrey Pines Mesa, bringing the first group of physicists to the region in 1955. Coincidentally, in that same year, the Scripps Clinic and Research Foundation, precursor to the present-day Scripps Research Institute (TSRI), was also founded on the Torrey Pines Mesa. In 1960, while all of this was going on, the mayor of San Diego convinced Jonas Salk to locate his new research institute on the Torrey Pines Mesa as well, with the promise of city lands donated to Salk for a dollar. The mayor had been a polio victim and greatly admired Salk's achievements in discovering a vaccine, and the work of the March of Dimes, which helped raise funding for research. The City of San Diego zoned additional land nearby in adjacent Sorrento Valley for commercial development. In so doing, in the early 1960s, they created a geographical zone with a small group of highly contiguous research institutions, each with a core of superstar scientists, which today has grown to more than fifty institutions and thousands of globally respected research scientists. [155]

At the time, the civic, academic, and business leaders of the community could not have envisioned what sort of commercial and research development would ultimately result. Furthermore, at the time, there were powerful, vested interests who wanted to see these valuable, large tracts of ocean-view property on the Torrey Pines Mesa developed for residential subdivisions or tourism. Because commercial land developers prevailed, the Torrey Pines Mesa offered nearby space for young companies to be established alongside the establishment of UC San Diego, a world-class university. The present-day proximity of the biotech and wireless-communications industries to UC San Diego and the other research institutions on the Torrey Pines Mesa is a direct result of these prescient decisions related to land use and zoning, made decades before the industry clusters arose.

2. Building globally competitive research institutions from the ground up. UC San Diego, The Scripps Research Institute (TSRI), and Salk are still relatively young institutions, founded between 1955 and 1960. The Sanford-Burnham Medical Research Institute is even younger, having been founded in 1976. The founders of these institutions envisioned the creation of world-class institutions and, thanks to the private and public resources, were able to attract world-class talent to San Diego. Today, the combined research budgets of the institutes on the Torrey Pines Mesa is close to $2 billion annually. While the private-sector supporters hoped the University of California would train engineers for the growing defense industry in San Diego, university founders at the Scripps Institution of Oceanography, including Revelle, envisioned a campus led by the new physics and biology advances of that era, including the discovery of DNA as the building block of life. TSRI, Salk, and then Burnham were founded with similarly lofty aspirations. UC San Diego, in its early days, focused on attracting senior-level research talent, and in building superior research facilities, not on applied sciences, technology commercialization, or spin-off companies. The other young institutes on the Torrey Pines Mesa engaged in a similar strategy.

In contrast to most U.S. universities, UC San Diego started life in 1960 as a graduate school of science and engineering, focused on research in physics and biology. Undergraduates arrived later, as did the growth of UC San Diego as a general university encompassing arts, humanities, social sciences, and medicine, in addition to the basic sciences, engineering, and oceanography. The founding science faculty recruited by Revelle and others included two Nobel Laureates and 13 National Academy of Science members, all risk-taking intellectual mavericks and leaders in their fields. These academic stars were the entrepreneurial scientists of their time. In Revelle's own words:

> *"...starting a new physics department, in a non-existent university, in a remote resort town, where [one] would be surrounded by oceanographers, was just the kind of far-out gamble that [these researchers] would be completely unable to resist."* [156]

Faculty who accepted positions at UC San Diego brought with them funded grants, graduate students, and lab equipment. Since they were all world-class researchers with proven ability to win outside the university funding for their work, UC San Diego shot up rapidly in the university rankings. Indeed, as Revelle later said, "Attracting superstars is the cheapest way to start a research university."

Simultaneously, Salk, TSRI, and General Atomics were doing the same thing, so that by the late 1970s, La Jolla was developing a global reputation as a major center of basic research.

3. A local culture of collaboration between academic, public, and private sectors.
The San Diego region has a long history of collaboration between the academic, public, and private sectors, going back over one hundred years, with the Chamber of Commerce's efforts to get the U.S. Navy and the U.S. Army Corps of Engineers to dredge San Diego harbor and make it amenable for commercial shipping. The Chamber of Commerce was again involved in 1902 with other local boosters and Dr. William Ritter, a University of California zoologist from Berkeley, in creating the Marine Biological Association of San Diego and lobbying the University of California to create a permanent Marine Biological Station in La Jolla, the precursor of the Scripps Institution of Oceanography. Half a century later, were it not for the private interests associated with the Chamber of Commerce lobbying for the founding of the university in the early 1950s following a period of economic crisis, the San Diego City Council would not have made the land-use and zoning decisions for the Torrey Pines Mesa that ultimately affected the location of not just UC San

Diego, but the Scripps Research Institute, the Salk Institute for Biological Studies, and the General Atomics facility as well.

In the early 1980s, during another period of regional economic downturn and crisis, the private sector again rallied a major commitment of time and resources to engage with the research community. Business and economic-development leaders recognized that their repeated efforts at business attraction and their attempts to bring large research consortia (e.g., MCC and SEMATECH) to San Diego had failed. This time, it was the regional economic-development corporation that led the conversation with UC San Diego leadership, to find a solution to the regional economic malaise. The result of that dialogue was the commitment by UC San Diego to organize a self-funded program to support high-tech entrepreneurs and science-based companies in the San Diego region. In 1985, UC San Diego CONNECT was founded by a small group of local supporters, including the San Diego Regional Economic Development Corporation, local-business service providers, and two successful early high-tech entrepreneurs: Irwin Jacobs, then the ex-CEO of Linkabit, a consulting firm that he had founded prior to Qualcomm, and David Hale, CEO of Hybritech, San Diego's first biotech firm, along with UC San Diego's deans of Engineering and Extension.

4. Continuous private sector commitment to support the commercialization efforts of UC San Diego. The Bayh-Dole Act was passed by Congress just prior to UC San Diego CONNECT's founding in 1985, so there had been minimal technology-transfer activity at UC San Diego prior to the 1980s. In fact, UC San Diego did not have a technology-transfer office on campus until 1995, as these services had been centrally provided by the UC system-wide Office of Technology Transfer. UC San Diego CONNECT was, therefore, a unique technology-commercialization partnership between the business and academic community to engage UC San Diego in regional-development efforts. Private-sector commitment to UC San Diego CONNECT went beyond financial support for its programs. Private-sector CEOs and senior partners from local-business service providers (bankers, lawyers, and accountants) gave freely of their time to mentor technology entrepreneurs starting high-tech and biotech companies. Extensive interviews with senior university leadership of that era, as well as some of CONNECT's early supporters reveal that both university and private-sector leadership learned from these early encounters how to engage with each other for mutual benefit. These early relationships formed a basis of trust which, over time, enabled the extensive industrial partnerships that underlie UC San Diego's and the region's many multidisciplinary research institutes such as the California Institute for Telecommunications and Information Technology (Calit2), the California Institute for Regenerative Medicine, and the Center for Wireless Health.

5. A powerful sense of place that binds all inhabitants. San Diego County has a physical geography that separates it from the rest of California and is distinctive in the United States. The Mexican border lies to the south; the Pacific Ocean lies to the west; the Peninsular Range of mountains defines the eastern border; and a large Marine base, Camp Pendleton, separates the county from the Los Angeles/Orange County sprawl to the north. This physical isolation has defined San Diego as a place for more than two centuries and bound its inhabitants together in a way that distinguishes San Diegans from the rest of California. Because of this seeming isolation in the southwestern-most corner of the United States, there is a powerful "sense of place," if only for lifestyle, that binds both old, established San Diegans as well as newly arrived transplants to the region. This "sense of place" creates common incentives among San Diegans for making things work, helping new initiatives and enterprises start and succeed, often through an investment of personal time, connections, and cash.

There is also a set of norms and values reinforcing the idea that everyone would be worse off if San Diegans were not to collaborate for the common economic good. Successive generations of San Diegans had learned that for the region to remain vibrant, all interested parties must pool resources in order to support new and uncertain ventures through shared agenda-setting, shared investment, shared risks, and shared rewards. Institutional mechanisms (e.g., CONNECT) have grown up to facilitate the creation of the trust relationships that are essential to sharing investments and pooling resources. Add to this the temperate climate and physical beauty of the region, and what results is that talent and wealth stay in the region. This, in turn, forges links between the early entrepreneurs and the multiple generations of progeny companies, with time and dollars reinvested in new enterprises.

The growing concentration of wealth and reinvestment in the region is also reflected by the growth in local philanthropy. Over the past thirty years, close to a billion dollars' worth of new philanthropic funds has been established through a variety of family and regional-community foundations. This new personal and corporate philanthropy has greatly benefited the many research institutes on the Torrey Pines Mesa and especially the UC San Diego campus, in terms of endowed chairs, scholarship support, and multimillion-dollar gifts for facilities and capital improvements. It has greatly facilitated the excellence of schools at UC San Diego, including the Graduate School of International Relations and Pacific Studies, the Jacobs School of Engineering, the Skaggs School of Pharmacy and Pharmaceutical Sciences, and the Rady School of Management. Furthermore, the establishment of collaborative interdisciplinary programs with other research institutes across the Torrey Pines Mesa has similarly benefited from the increase in philanthropy fueled by the phenomenal success of San Diego's high-tech clusters. A particularly useful example of this is the CONNECT program launched by UC San Diego in 1985.

HOW SAN DIEGO BUILT ITS INNOVATION AND COMMERCIALIZATION CAPACITY [157]

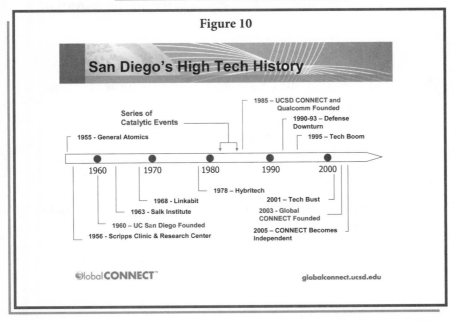

Figure 10

San Diego's High Tech History

Series of Catalytic Events

1985 – UCSD CONNECT and Qualcomm Founded
1990-93 – Defense Downturn
1995 – Tech Boom

1955 - General Atomics

1960   1970   1980   1990   2000

1978 – Hybritech
1968 - Linkabit   2001 – Tech Bust
1963 - Salk Institute   2003 - Global CONNECT Founded
1960 – UC San Diego Founded
1956 - Scripps Clinic & Research Center   2005 – CONNECT Becomes Independent

GlobalCONNECT™   globalconnect.ucsd.edu

The journey from a promising idea to a useful technology that solves a real problem in a manner that is scalable, affordable, and marketable is what technology commercialization is about. It goes beyond issues of patenting and knowledge transfer and focuses squarely on testing, demonstrating, validating, and, ultimately, translating a promising idea into a useful and marketable product. It is a journey that Duane Roth, the current CEO of CONNECT, describes as the four 'D's; discovery research, defining a potential application, developing and validating the application, delivering the solution to a market.[158] For this to occur, a number of conditions are necessary and a variety of competencies are essential, all of which are captured by the CONNECT model developed through trial and error at UC San Diego in the 1980s. An active focus on technology commercialization enabled by the CONNECT model can result in a rapid growth of robust science-based company clusters such as those established in IT, life science, software, clean technology, and innovative sports, in San Diego in recent decades. These clusters of companies have created tens of thousands of high-wage jobs, new tax revenues, and personal wealth, which, combined, have been a powerful driver of regional economic development.

Effective commercialization systems such as the CONNECT program in San Diego are enabled by five critical elements:

1. **Cross-professional knowledge relevant to innovation:**

    - Tech-savvy business community
    - Business-savvy science community

2. **An experimental, risk-oriented culture adept at managing uncertainty:**

    - Discovery, experimental, and entrepreneurial and science

    - Nimble business culture and practices, i.e., entrepreneurial business know-how

3. **Platforms through which these two communities connect:**

    - Integrative mechanisms that enable frequent pre-transactional interactions between business and science

- Increased trust and a shared sense of purpose

4. **The presence of honest brokers and multiple gateways to increase frequency/diversity of interaction:**

- Knowledge flows and trust building
- Rapid and numerous application and commercialization activities
- More proven products, successful companies, new jobs, and new wealth

5. **A culture of reinvestment:**

Successful entrepreneurs and entrepreneurial teams share their know-how and support others by:

- Sharing knowledge and relationships

- Contributing time

- Investing personal cash in new ventures

- Providing access to capital for promising ventures

- Contributing to regional institutions through philanthropy

- Seeking a return on involvement, meaningful tasks with visible outcomes that benefit the region as well as themselves

Each of these elements deserves further description with specific examples from the San Diego experience.

CROSS-PROFESSIONAL KNOWLEDGE RELEVANT TO INNOVATION

The University of California campus in San Diego was established in the late 1950s and opened its doors to Ph.D. students in 1960. The growth strategy was to build a cadre of senior-level faculty across a number of academic disciplines in order to attract the best and the brightest, and to quickly build a research university. In the early years, the faculty brought with it significant research grants and was a magnet for excellent graduate students and post-docs, so that by the time the campus opened its doors to freshmen, it already had a small but distinguished, well-funded research faculty in place. This faculty was made up of basic scientists with minimal interest in industrial relations or technology commercialization.

A small number of the early faculty members, however, were involved in research areas that had promising applications in the solution of real-world problems. Notable among these were:

- Irwin Jacobs, professor of electrical engineering and computer science, who consulted the U.S. Navy on remote-signal processing, and refined the CDMA technology platform that became the basis for the founding of the company Linkabit in the early 1970s and Qualcomm in the mid-1980s.

- Ivor Royston, professor of medicine, who worked in the groundbreaking field of monoclonal antibodies in cancer research and founded Hybritech in the early 1970s, in large part because he needed cell samples for his research lab.

The success of Linkabit and Hybritech, less than twenty years after the founding of the university, created a buzz in the San Diego region that led people to believe it might be possible to grow robust clusters of high-technology companies on the model of Silicon Valley.

Simultaneous with the growth of the UC San Diego campus and these early company successes that built upon the entrepreneurial energies of two professors, came a recession in California that had profound and troubling effects in San Diego. The savings and loan crisis of the early 1980s, the increasing competitiveness of European and Asian nations in R&D, shifting investments by the Department of Defense, unsuccessful attempts in the early 1980s to attract major companies or research consortia to the region, combined with rising unemployment, created a deep concern about where the region's economic future would lie. As a result, a group of civic leaders led by the San Diego Regional Economic Development Corporation (who were not especially sophisticated about science and technology, but were aware of some of the early individual company successes associated with the young University of California campus), asked Chancellor Richard C.

Atkinson to identify ways in which the campus might be more of a partner in regional economic development. Atkinson had been a professor at Stanford for more than twenty years, and after that, the director of the prestigious National Science Foundation for six years. He had worked closely with Senators Birch Bayh and Bob Dole to develop the legislation that enabled the commercialization of federally funded research. He was highly responsive to these community overtures and dispatched a small group of university colleagues to investigate what might be possible.

One of the authors of this book, Mary Walshok, had just been appointed the dean of the university's Extension division and, as a research sociologist, thanks to a Kellogg Foundation fellowship, had been doing interviews in the Silicon Valley to understand the dynamics of innovation in that region. Based on knowledge of the dynamics of Silicon Valley and interviews with key supporters in San Diego, a brief report was prepared for the chancellor and a few key stakeholders, describing what the community needed to do to build on the successes of early start-up companies such as Linkabit and Hybritech in order to grow robust clusters of science and technology companies similar to those in the Silicon Valley.

It was at this time that the core concept of the CONNECT program emerged. When the scientists and engineers who started successful companies were interviewed, their primary emphasis was on the need for a more responsive, nimble, and technology-savvy business community. In the late 1970s and early 1980s, engineers and scientists who became company entrepreneurs secured their funding, their legal services, their accounting, and marketing services outside of San Diego because of the absence of professional services (e.g. – intellectual property attorneys, venture capital firms, international marketing consultants) community capable of responding to their distinctive needs. Of particular note was the need for service providers with some understanding of technology, intellectual property, and the risk cycles involved with start-ups, as well as global regulatory and marketing challenges. San Diego had been a community characterized by tourism, agriculture, and defense contracting and therefore lacked a business community capable of working with the entrepreneurial scientists who were aggregating around the UC San Diego campus and the other research institutions on the Torrey Pines Mesa.

In contrast, when local business leaders were asked about what they felt would be needed to grow robust science-based clusters, they predictably emphasized the need for scientists and engineers to become more sophisticated about the real costs of producing particular technology solutions, to develop a clearer sense of the market for their technologies, and to be willing to work with professional managers in realizing the potential of their technology, particularly through a profitable business. In other words, they needed business skills.

These two contrasting views of pressing needs actually became two interlocking themes in all of the developments within CONNECT over the next twenty-five years. Everyone today recognizes that innovation in the science and technology space is supported by an ecosystem of complementary competencies and resources. What was distinctive about the CONNECT program in the 1980s was that, mirroring the success of the Silicon Valley, it was set up to become the hub or connective link within that ecosystem of innovation for the San Diego region. The founding members' mission and goals, represented in a one-page statement, reflected these two themes:

- The need to develop more science and technology product-development sophistication among the business community.

- The need to develop more financial, marketing, and management intelligence among the scientific community.

Today, through approximately three hundred annual programs focused on things such as "Meet the Researcher" for business people and "Global Strategies for Financing High-Tech Companies" for scientists and engineers, the CONNECT program continues to build the cross-professional knowledge networks essential for innovation.

A RISK-ORIENTED CULTURE ADEPT AT MANAGING UNCERTAINTY

The commercialization support efforts of the CONNECT program resulted in large numbers of companies securing venture capital. Fully three times as many CONNECT-assisted companies were still in business five years after receiving CONNECT support as other start-ups. This was helped by the rapidity with which the business community came to understand and respect the wide range of risky, cutting-edge research initiatives taking place on the Torrey Pines Mesa and the extent to which the scientists, due to their regular interactions with the business community, began to respect the competencies and resources the business community could bring to the commercialization process.

The entrepreneurial character of the research institutions across the Torrey Pines Mesa, shaped in the '60s and '70s by a culture of excellence, meshed well with the risk-enabling business culture CONNECT helped to cultivate. The recruitment strategies for faculty and researchers focused on bringing people who were at the front end of knowledge development and involved in highly interdisciplinary endeavors. The result was a significant infusion of federal and foundation dollars in a short time to the institutions across the Mesa and a growing identity of the region as being involved in breakthrough field-defining science. It is important to understand the extent to which one must be tenacious and entrepreneurial to secure the level of funding the scientists across the Torrey Pines Mesa were able to acquire. This is an entrepreneurial skill that not all research scientists at all research universities possess. It may be one of the differentiating characteristics of the scientists at the highest-performing research institutions. The business community understood early on that this was an unusual set of skills and they developed profound respect for this kind of science. It helped that many of the early companies, though not direct spin-offs from UC San Diego or Salk, involved faculty and researchers working in those institutions. It was also the result of the articulate leadership of Chancellor Atkinson and the wide range of early programs sponsored by CONNECT that celebrated good science and fundamental research.

At the same time, the business community, which included law firms, accounting firms, marketing firms, and even real-estate developers, was becoming more sophisticated in their entrepreneurial skills and relationships. Within a decade of the founding of CONNECT, dozens of law firms in the region formed strategic partnerships with intellectual-property law firms from other parts of the country. The various venture forums sponsored by CONNECT in its early years resulted in many venture funds establishing offices in the San Diego region. A number of national marketing firms with technology clients and experience in global markets opened offices or formed strategic alliances with local marketing firms. Within a decade, a genuinely risk-oriented culture adept at managing the uncertainties involved in incubating R & D start-ups became firmly established in the region. By the mid-1990s, growth in company formations, venture-capital funding, and IPOs grew exponentially.

INTEGRATIVE PLATFORMS

A fundamental concept in sociology is that frequent interaction between people and groups increases understanding and affection. George Homans, a leading theoretical sociologist at Harvard University, asserted this sociological principle decades ago and empirical evidence supports it.[159] CONNECT represents an integrative mechanism, a platform for activities that increase interactions between previously isolated communities. Any innovation ecosystem needs a place where diverse community interests, knowledge bases, and resources can connect. This ecosystem evolved slowly in Silicon Valley and along the Route 128 corridor in Massachusetts. Since the 1980s, however, it has been enabled and facilitated by university-aligned programs such as IC2 at the University of Texas, Austin; the Council for Entrepreneurial Development in the North Carolina Research Triangle Park; and CONNECT on the Torrey Pines Mesa in La Jolla.

These platforms represent more than just a collection of networking activities and events. They involve stakeholders in a variety of meaningful interactions that produce three sets of benefits:

- They organize activities that harvest experience and knowledge in the region in a manner that can truly help both the scientist seeking validation for an idea, and the entrepreneur seeking input on a business plan.

- They occur in a setting that is pre-transactional and completely open. Ideas and plans can be discussed, criticized, and adapted in a highly collegial manner in advance of an "official" presentation for angel capital, the development of a business plan for venture capital, or corporate partnering. To this end, a culture emerges in which ideas are not stolen and side deals are not made and, as a consequence, people feel free to share their knowledge in an open manner.

- The nature of the interaction is such that people learn not only about specific technologies or business plans, but about one another. That is how a community of innovation and a culture of shared risk can evolve. In surveying members who contribute endless hours to various CONNECT mentoring, evaluation, and education programs, one hears again and again that, "I participate in these programs as much for what I learn about my colleagues as because of the exposure to new ideas and new business plans. Familiarizing myself with the 'personalities' as well as the capabilities and client lists of my peers in the business community helps me put together teams in the future that work for the companies I'm supporting." The events and activities sponsored by a commercializing platform need to have these key characteristics.

The upshot is an enormous amount of information sharing and resource sharing among a large and diverse group of stakeholders. The comment one often hears at various CONNECT events is, "I can't personally help you but I have a friend or a colleague who's very good at this." Or, "There's no one in San Diego who's working in this particular space, but I have a good friend in Seattle who is supporting a company of this nature. Let me get his name to you immediately." This spirit of not just knowledge sharing but resource and relationship sharing is absolutely critical in connecting the two communities.

The close interactions between CONNECT and the technology-transfer offices from the various research institutions on the Torrey Pines Mesa helps mitigate against the potential dangers of sharing an idea before it is patented. The other benefit of the platform is that it becomes a receptor community for many of the promising patents and licensing arrangements coming out of the various technology-transfer offices across the research institutions on the Torrey Pines Mesa. Protection of intellectual property is absolutely critical once an idea or application is defined as having real promise. The journey through the testing and validation of the idea or application and the exploration of its viability in terms of production, marketing, and pricing, however, is the longer journey in the commercialization process for which the CONNECT platform has proven so valuable. It is for this reason that traditional technology-transfer offices work so closely and effectively with the CONNECT program.

MULTIPLE GATEWAYS

Above and beyond the existence of the CONNECT program as an integrative platform that draws in the knowledge and resources of both the entrepreneurial science community and the entrepreneurial business community, there is enormous value in having multiple gateways through which science and business can interact. CONNECT learned early on that it did not need to be the gatekeeper, the central door through which all industry interactions, including tech transfer, should occur, but rather one of many honest brokers in the ecosystem. Once again, recent research bears out the value of multiple points of entry in a knowledge-creating community. The frequency and diversity of interaction through industrial affiliate programs, technology-commercialization initiatives, entrepreneurship education in schools of engineering, and nimble offices of technology transfer, results in knowledge flowing in many directions and results in faster and more effective application, development, and commercialization of promising research initiatives. Universities such as UC San Diego and Stanford have dozens of offices located in multiple departments and schools through which industry interactions occur. These represent an important part of the innovation equation because of the ease with which people can have access to the knowledge that ultimately produces products, companies, jobs, and wealth, as well as the capability to accelerate the rate of start-ups.

The UC San Diego example is instructive. CONNECT was founded before there was a Technology Transfer Office at UC San Diego, and simultaneous with the establishment of the first Industrial Affiliates Program at UC San Diego. At the time CONNECT was founded, there were no technology-industry groups in the San Diego region except for the American Electronics Association whose members were engineers drawn primarily from defense-contracting businesses. CONNECT, in its first decade, became the platform through which a variety of campus-based industrial affiliates programs were formed and a number of industry-specific advocacy groups were spun out, in particular, BIOCOM and the Regional Technology Alliance. CONNECT has been a strategic partner in the development of the William J. von Liebig Center for Entrepreneurism and Technology Advancement within the Jacobs School of Engineering, the clinical-research initiatives at the School of Medicine, and a variety of other independent but aligned activities at UC San Diego.

Multiple gateways matter. A commercialization platform is critical, but a commercialization platform that engages all of the various paths to knowledge development and technology connections is essential. The CONNECT program differs from many other commercialization efforts throughout the United States and the world by being part of the ecosystem, not on top of it, or the exclusive gateway to it. As such, it benefits enormously from lots of good ideas and business-development opportunities flowing into its offices from multiple sources. The most recent data on high-tech-company formation in San Diego indicates that a new high-tech company is started every seventeen hours. This is a sign that the highly fluid ecosystem of innovation is working effectively (see Figure 11).

Figure 11
Number of Innovation Start-ups:
Change by Quarter, Q1 2007 – Q4 2009

	2007				2008				2009			
	1st Qtr.	2nd Qtr.	3rd Qtr.	4th Qtr.	1st Qtr.	2nd Qtr.	3rd Qtr.	4th Qtr.	1st Qtr.	2nd Qtr.	3rd Qtr.	4th Qtr.
# of Innovation Start-ups	49	64	105	149	47	76	103	72	66	102	78	74
% Change from Previous Quarter		31%	64%	42%	-68%	62%	36%	-30%	-8%	55%	-24%	-5%
% Change from Previous Year					-4%	19%	-2%	-52%	40%	34%	-24%	3%

Source: CONNECT

A CULTURE OF REINVESTMENT

A final characteristic of highly successful commercialization systems and, especially, university-aligned programs such as CONNECT, is the culture of reinvestment. Successful entrepreneurs (whether they are scientists or business people) and the teams they develop share their know-how and make a commitment to growing the innovation culture of which they are a part. Based on the extraordinary involvement of literally hundreds of scientists and business people from the San Diego region in the various programs of CONNECT, it is possible to describe the ways in which this culture of reinvestment expresses itself.

It begins with a sharing of knowledge and relationships that can be mobilized to support the work of relatively unknown and untried individuals and ideas. Through mentoring, seminars, workshops, and interactive roundtables, experienced professionals and scientists share their knowledge with less-experienced people and are generous in their efforts to help make connections that contribute to success. This type of sharing involves significant contributions of personal time by a wide range of individuals. In the case of CONNECT, these individuals are not simply successful entrepreneurs with discretionary time and money to mentor and support new business ventures. Participants include a large number of well-educated, highly seasoned professionals whose typical billable hour represents hundreds of dollars. Through the CONNECT program, these individuals contribute their time, wisdom, and experience on a pro bono basis.

Reinvestment also involves cash. CONNECT was the incubator for the formation of an angel investment group known as the Tech Coast Angels that today numbers more than 140 individuals. Using the offices of CONNECT and sharing support staff, the Tech Coast Angels meet at the UC San Diego Faculty Club once a month for briefings on exciting new developments in which angel investment can make a difference. This group includes a wide array of individuals with diverse business backgrounds (retired attorneys and bankers, successful real-estate developers, and savvy high-tech entrepreneurs). In addition to the involvement of early-stage angel investors in the commercialization process, equally important is access to institutional sources of capital such as venture capital and corporate partnering. Successful entrepreneurs and experienced, well-connected business service providers in the region are often bridges to major sources of capital for new companies. Through these individuals, doors are constantly being opened for the young, the unknown, or spin-off teams from established companies.

Finally, one of the most interesting things about the San Diego region and the role of CONNECT in the region is the extraordinary growth in philanthropy over the last thirty years. The vast majority of new philanthropic funds are in personal foundations, family foundations, and community foundations, which have come from the wealth created by successful science and technology entrepreneurs in the region. Hundreds of millions of dollars in new funds have been established and much has been contributed to the university in the form of endowed chairs, fellowships, and financial support for promising graduate students, as well as for buildings and physical facilities. CONNECT often acts as a partner in the development of these resources and played a leadership role in the growth of endowed chairs at the university, the establishment of the new Rady School of Management at UC San Diego, the formation of the San Diego Consortium for Regenerative Medicine involving four research institutions on the Torrey Pines Mesa, as well as support for K–12 charter schools focused on developing the pipeline of math and science talent. This spirit of philanthropy and culture of reinvestment has been critical for the continued success of the university and leading research institutions on the Mesa, as well as for the growth of robust clusters of innovative science-based companies in the San Diego region.

Surveys of the pro bono participants and investors in many of the CONNECT activities reveal that people are looking for two kinds of return on investment. Clearly, business development is one of the things that motivates participation. Return on involvement and participation is as important as return in financial terms. Because the commercialization strategies developed by CONNECT involve meaningful tasks with visible outcomes that benefit the region as well as the individual participants, there is a sense of contributing to civic well-being by becoming a part of the CONNECT network. CONNECT's efforts are enhanced by the membership fees and program underwriting support so generously provided by a wide range of businesses across the region. It is also the personal involvement of hundreds of professionals and scientists that makes the CONNECT program work. Annually, the CONNECT program sponsors close to three hundred different events and activities and secures program fees, membership fees, underwriting, and $3 million in private-sector philanthropic support. It receives no public or university funding for any of its staff or activities, nor does it receive city, county, or state funding. It is a fully self-supporting, community-engaging technology-commercialization initiative characterized by a strong culture of reinvestment.

The results of these multiple efforts are summed up in the quarterly Innovation Report on San Diego prepared by CONNECT.[160] Even during the years of the worst recession in recent history, the region's innovation activity has been impressive (see Figures 12–16).

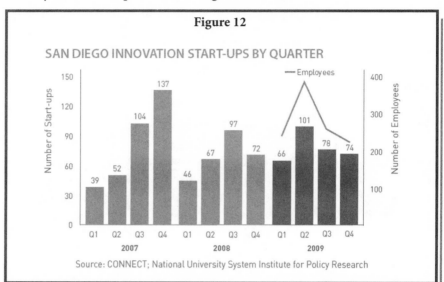

Figure 12

SAN DIEGO INNOVATION START-UPS BY QUARTER

Source: CONNECT; National University System Institute for Policy Research

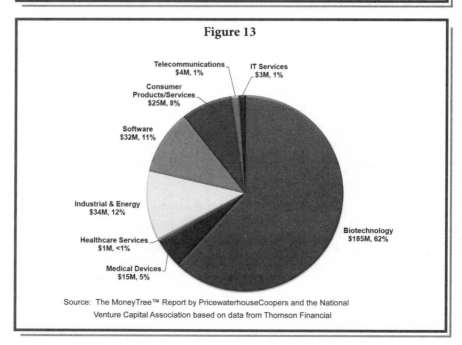

Figure 13

Source: The MoneyTree™ Report by PricewaterhouseCoopers and the National Venture Capital Association based on data from Thomson Financial

Figure 14
Patents Granted to San Diego County Organizations in 2009

Rank	Institution	Patents Granted
1	QUALCOMM Incorporated	247
2	Broadcom Corporation (San Diego group)	81
3	Callaway Golf Company	79
4	Hewlett-Packard Development Company, L.P.	64
5	Sony Corporation	63
6	Sony Electronics Inc.	59
7	The Regents of the University of California	54
8	Acushnet Company	45
9	Kyocera Wireless Corp.	41
10	Taylor Made Golf Company, Inc.	39
11	Sun Microsystems, Inc.	37
12	The Scripps Research Institute	34
13	Nokia Corporation	22
14	SPAWAR Systems Center	21
15	Cymer, Inc.	20
15	Isis Pharmaceuticals, Inc.	20
15	Janssen Pharmaceutica N.V.	20

Source: United States Patent and Trademark Organization; University of California, San Diego; CONNECT.

Figure 15
Federal Research Grants Received in San Diego – 2009 Summary

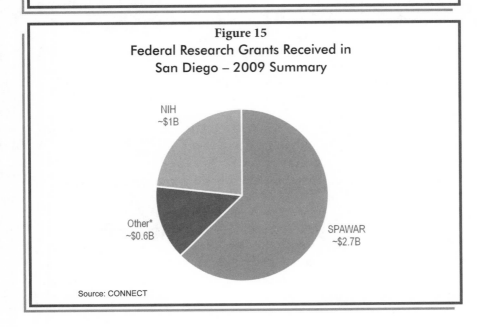

NIH ~$1B

Other* ~$0.6B

SPAWAR ~$2.7B

Source: CONNECT

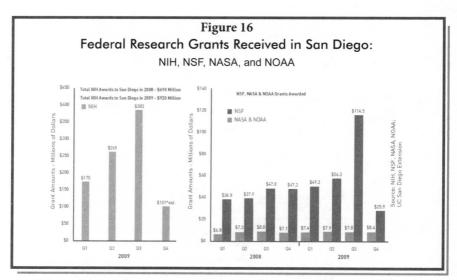

Figure 16
Federal Research Grants Received in San Diego:
NIH, NSF, NASA, and NOAA

These impressive outcomes are a function of frequent interactions among multiple stakeholders in San Diego's innovation economy. Thoughtful examination of what enables knowledge transfer, technology commercialization, and, ultimately, new-business formation and job creation was summed up nicely by Robert C. Miller and Bernard J. Le Boeuf in their 2008 book of case studies on university–industry relations.[161] They identify nine principles of practice within research institutes and universities which enable the growth of innovation in a region:

1. Build relationships and enhance goodwill.

2. Extend the teaching mission of the university by deploying technologies developed in the course of university research into the private sector.

3. Encourage and develop entrepreneurs in the university.

4. Ensure that both faculty and students are knowledgeable and comfortable with any negotiated agreement.

5. Communicate the objectives of the university, faculty, and students early in discussions with prospective company partners.

6. Make the mission of industry liaison-tech transfer clear and provide appropriate resources.

7. Develop metrics of success that reflect all aspects of university–industry affairs.

8. Support an integrated approach to the management of university–industry affairs.

9. Economic development should be viewed realistically and valued as a role for the university.

So, fine, you say. You've described how research capacity and community-supported commercialization efforts create innovation, but what about the job-creation piece? The ramifications for both policymakers and employers are the subject of chapter 6.

CHAPTER 6

The Good News for America: The Gap Can Be Closed

theme of this book is that the dream of good jobs for all is alive and well; that is, if America invests the time to understand what is really going on and then undertakes informed action. Section One of this book began with an examination of America's job gap, the disparity between the good jobs being created by small-business innovation in the U.S. and the lack of American workers with the skills to fill these good jobs. The weight of the data clearly demonstrates something is terribly amiss with projections of economic recovery and the disproportionate job growth.

Section Two began with the concept that a region other than Silicon Valley can and should use innovation to create good jobs and community prosperity. Now we turn our attention to policymakers, entrepreneurs, and company leaders, and what they can do to close the job gap for the country and for their companies, and their individual situations in a turbulent world. Today's constant is change. The sheer volume of knowledge is now doubling every five years. Thanks to computer connectivity, once-thriving hometown economies are being forced by global forces and market opportunities to adapt or suffer the consequences. Goods and services can be developed, bought, sold, and, in many cases, even delivered over electronic networks at the speed of light. The impact of daily shifts in technology and global developments on civic, company, and personal decisions can be tremendous. Lifelong learning makes a significant contribution to increasing productivity and improving the employment rate. Adult education raises the overall quality of the talent pool, prevents professional qualifications from becoming obsolete, and helps career-advancers find better jobs. Up-to-date citizens also make better decisions and lead richer lives. In short, investing in lifelong learning is a requirement for the knowledge-based economy. Unlike other investments, knowledge is always an appreciating asset. To quote the great innovator Benjamin Franklin, "If a man empties his purse into his head, no man can take it away from him. An investment in knowledge always pays the best interest"

IMPLICATIONS FOR PUBLIC POLICY

Policymakers have a vital role to play in closing America's job gap. Following are some of the implications of the need for job creation and reskilling of workers for public policy, economic-development strategies, and civic leadership.

Due to rising global competition, America's capacity for generating stable, well-paying jobs is at risk. In today's environment, regions need to be thinking about the industry clusters that can harness their assets to grow innovative new enterprises that can contribute to job creation. The federal government is positioned to enable locally driven cluster initiatives, and regional business leaders and elected public officials need to be sure that they do so. Now is the time to align federal programs to maximize the resources provided to each region. The time also has come for more ongoing conversations and strategic thinking between economic- and business-development associations, the research and innovation community, and the education and training providers across the region. Our long-term competitiveness and prosperity depend on it.

Business clusters have existed throughout American history. Naturally occurring clusters—like Detroit's auto industry; Akron, Ohio's tire plants; and Hollywood's film studios—all developed because of a combination of geographic and natural resources that were exploited by local inventors and entrepreneurs. These clusters produced more than cars, whitewalls, and hit movies: They created the demand for hundreds of smaller parts companies and services suppliers and produced thousands of jobs. Clusters like these evolved and grew over decades. However, the days of waiting for clusters to grow on their own have passed. In today's challenging economic times, Mother Nature could use a little help from human ingenuity and even Uncle Sam.

The economist Richard Florida has found that some regions capitalize on their unique assets to attract skilled workers and new businesses.[162] Many regions of the United States have already developed into epicenters of particular occupations and industries, producing abundant good jobs. These include:

- Computers in Boston
- Fashion design in New York City
- Marine engineers in Virginia Beach, Virginia
- Recreation in Orlando, Florida
- Real estate in Miami
- Medicine in Philadelphia
- Music in Nashville
- Petroleum in Houston
- Semiconductors in Austin, Texas
- Gaming in Las Vegas, Nevada
- Wineries in Napa, California
- Textiles in Anderson, South Carolina

As previously mentioned, San Diego witnessed this organic phenomenon with the growth of both wireless IT and the life-sciences clusters that sprang up along the Torrey Pines Mesa adjacent to UC San Diego. The community networks that included university researchers, venture-capital firms, government, workforce organizations, and catalysts like UC San Diego CONNECT have been largely responsible for the robust growth and success of these clusters. And San Diego continues to grow innovative clusters in new and converging technologies such as clean technology, health-care IT, and biofuels.

In recent years, many government and industry organizations across the globe have turned to this concept of coordinated economic development as a means to stimulate urban and regional economic growth. As a result, a large number of cluster initiative organizations were started during the 1990s, and the trend continues.

Central governments in advanced countries have launched numerous programs to promote growth-producing collaboration in key industry clusters. In fact, twenty-six of thirty-one European Union countries have cluster initiative programs, as do Japan and Korea. The United States does not.

Even in collaborative San Diego there is no platform that regularly brings together the four key players: the research community, which is developing the technologies that will shape the businesses and jobs of the future; the entrepreneurs and investors, who can turn a promising technology into a business; the economic developers, who focus on the use of resource allocation and business policies that can assure economic prosperity; and the educators and workforce-training organizations, which focus on the general and specialized skills needed in globally competitive industries and services.

Some observers point out that there are several other excellent federal economic and workforce programs in place, including the Department of Commerce's community-based job-training grants, the National Science Foundation's educational grants, and the Department of Labor's Education and Training Administration which funds, among other things, the services provided by local workforce partnerships. The problem is, for the most part, they operate in splendid isolation from one another at the federal level. At the local level, there are few incentives to create integrative platforms through which multiple voices can be heard and synergistic initiatives that produce commercialization, business growth, and job creation, can take place. This region needs and deserves such a place.

Karen Mills, author of a Brookings Institution paper on cluster initiatives, concurs that the federal government should be pressed to do more to promote clusters.[163] "Federal understanding of and interest in the economic competitiveness of all regions has been minimal," says Mills. "Existing development programs rarely reflect an appreciation of the importance of institutional collaboration and the unique dynamics of clusters." The Brookings Institution report recommends that the federal government promote cluster development with a two-pronged approach: First, create a national information center to track cluster programs and study cluster dynamics. Second, establish a grants program to support regional and state clusters.

SUPPORT RESKILLING PROGRAMS

Policymakers at the federal and state level need to include adult learners in their education plans.

Where can a region, a business, an individual turn to keep pace? Great social and economic prosperity comes from integrating the collective knowledge of the university, community leaders, and professionals.

A common misconception holds many individuals and organizations back. They do not take full advantage of the shifting global realities because of a belief that learning culminates with a degree. Many individuals and organizational leaders believe that an undergraduate or advanced degree, coupled with on-the-job experience, will provide the knowledge and skills sufficient for a professional career spanning several decades.

In today's world that is no longer true. One of the reasons lifelong learning has become so critical is the acceleration of scientific and technological progress coupled with a globalizing economy. Knowledgeable workers have more choices and can contribute to accelerating a region's economic vitality.

Other benefits accrue from lifelong learning. In addition to improving the talent pool, continuing education helps individuals to enrich their lives, contribute to their communities, help their children, and prolong their active lives.

More programs like Wisconsin's Adult Student Initiative and the Pennsylvania's Workforce Advancement Grant for Education (WAGE) are needed.[164] The Wisconsin program is designed to increase the number of adult, nontraditional students pursuing advanced education. The initiative gives funding to the University of Wisconsin system to provide continuing education to meet the needs of the adult working population.

The Pennsylvania program also provides financial aid to adult students. WAGE bridges funding gaps, providing grants to less-than-half-time students and other adults who would not otherwise qualify for financial assistance.

TIME TO SHATTER THE HOURGLASS ECONOMY

The time has come to break the hourglass economy.

Remember the hourglass? An early device for measuring time, the hourglass consists of two glass bulbs connected by a narrow tube through which fine sand flows at a given rate. What is troubling today is the resurgence of the hourglass economy, with job growth concentrated at the top and at the bottom of the labor market while middle-income jobs are shrinking. After World War II, America became a more football-shaped economy (picture a football on a kicking tee) with broad job growth in the middle and scant job growth at the top and bottom. This was a big improvement over ancient pyramid-shaped economies, with almost everyone on the bottom in terms of income, and ever fewer as you moved toward the top.

The authors view hourglass economies as undesirable because they create far too few middle-class incomes, which are of social and economic importance, because a democratic republic needs a robust middle class. Sadly, this is not the current trend.

The recent meltdown of housing and financial services and the decline in manufacturing across the United States, combined with the slashing of jobs in every area from retail to social services, have erased our giddy memories of the go-go economic growth of the 1990s. The recent double-digit unemployment figure in America should force us to reassess the boom years and recognize the actual dramatic growth of income inequality and working-class income losses that happened during those years.

More important, the current economic crisis is our opportunity to return to a football economy. Stanford economist Paul Romer is credited with the witty quote "A crisis is a terrible thing to waste." America has seldom wasted its crises in the past, and now is not the time to start.

If America's goal is a healthy and sustainable innovation economy, then our aim should be a shared prosperity with much more in the middle and less at the top and on the bottom. We need incentives in the service sector for people to innovate, educate workers, take risks, and expand business.

IMPLICATIONS FOR ENTREPRENEURS AND COMPANY LEADERS

America does not have to wait for the government to save us. All individuals and small companies should think about how to reinvent themselves. America is blessed with research institutions and an educated talent pool, the keys to innovation.

This is not something to leave to big business. The small business is crucial to close America's job gap. The U.S. Census data reveals that 98 percent of all U.S. firms have fewer than one hundred employees. These firms employ 50 percent of the private-sector workforce, are responsible for over 97 percent of all exported goods, and generate the majority of innovations that come from the United States.

BENEFITS TO EMPLOYERS OF CONTINUING EDUCATION

Many employers are skeptical about investing in employee development. Why not, reason many executives, just hire employees with the skills to fill the jobs? That is a common miscalculation.

Two decades of private industry and academic research, summarized in 2010 by Tim Lohrentz of the National Network of Sector Partners, confirms that employee development can improve employer bottom-line profitability by increasing revenues and lowering expenses.[165] The measurements come from a variety of methods including surveys, questionnaires, interviews, focus groups, tests, observation, and performance records. A review of the employee-development literature reveals the links to profitability in the following five main ways:

- Increased ability to take advantage of innovation
- Increased rate of employee retention
- Reduced rate of employee absenteeism
- Increased quality of work or service
- Increased productivity

Continuing education can provide huge paybacks to companies. In 2003, the W.E. Upjohn Institute for Employee Research reported the benefits of employee development to companies are primarily increased productivity, employee retention, and customer satisfaction, which are all highly correlated to profitability.[166] For public companies, the stock market is another measure. The Milken Institute Review reported in 2004 that firms that made large investments in employee development outperformed the control group in stock prices.[167]

> **"Workers thrown out of shrinking sectors like construction, finance and retail lack the skills for growing fields like health care, data mining and accounting."**

Employers have a vested interest in retraining employees. The largest asset that any company has that does appear on the balance sheet is its workforce.

Here is a point-by-point breakdown of these five drivers of profitability:

1. Increased ability to take advantage of innovation, which can be measured by:

- Better team performance
- Improved capacity to cope with change in the workplace

Many employers are surprised by the following statistic: *BusinessWeek* magazine reported in 2009 that in the midst of the worst recession in fifty years, there are approximately three million jobs that employers are actively recruiting but cannot fill. That's more job openings than the entire population of Iowa. [168]

The article pointed out that a "help wanted" sign is actually a bad sign. Workers thrown out of shrinking sectors like construction, finance, and retail lack the skills for growing fields like health care, data mining, and accounting. That is why the nation has millions of jobs that go begging to be filled. Without retraining, U.S. workers may not be able to fill them and take advantage of innovation. So is this just a matter of paying higher wages to find the necessary talent? No, concludes *BusinessWeek*. "Some jobs require specialized skills for which no amount of money will generate higher labor supply until a new generation can be trained."

2. Increased rate of employee retention, which can be measured by:

- Savings in recruitment and hiring
- Increases in job satisfaction
- Increases in customer satisfaction (for direct-service industries)

Employees greatly appreciate education benefits. In 2008 *HR World* magazine reported on a study conducted by Spherion Atlantic Enterprises LLC, a staffing firm, in which six out of ten respondents who received training or mentoring said they were very likely to remain with their current employer for the next five years.[169] Naturally, good employees are more likely to stick with a company when the employer is funding or helping to fund their continuing education. A large employer fear is that retraining employees is just preparing them to take a higher-paying job elsewhere. But that is not the case. In 2005 a study was released revealing that when examining a larger longitudinal worker survey, the researchers found that employees who received company training had a job-separation rate that is 8 percent lower than individuals with no such training.[170]

3. Reduced rate of employee absenteeism

The Conference Board reported that in a survey of five hundred CEOs, 98 percent reported at least one business benefit from workplace training.

One-third reported a reduction in absenteeism, and another 40 percent said that workplace training led to increased employee retention.[171]

4. Increased quality of work or service, which can be measured by:

- Decline in waste
- Decline in product rejection or error rate
- Increase in customer satisfaction or retention
- Better health and safety record

AAs innovation impacts all fields, continuing education is an excellent way to offer employees a chance to learn new technologies. Skills need to be updated, modernized, and developed to best suit the needs of the organization. If a company wants to grow and thrive, it should not solely rely on the skills its employees arrived with in today's competitive business world.

A 2003 study from The Aspen Institute found studies in its literature review that correlated employee training with reduced production-error rates.[172] A more recent study found that 92 percent of firms participating in a Massachusetts training program in 2008 reported increases in quality, and 91 percent reported increased productivity. [173]

5. Increased productivity, which can be measured by:

- Less time spent per task or per unit
- Increased output of products or services
- Time savings for managers and supervisors
- Improved capacity to use new technology

Studies from the United Kingdom show that training has a positive impact on productivity, with some companies gaining up to an 80-percent increase in productivity that can be attributed to training.[174] Increasing the proportion of employees trained by 5 percent is linked to a 4-percent increase in productivity in the UK.

More educated employees are more valuable employees. Following is an example suggested by the Web site Helium.com.[175] "Often it is less expensive to educate an existing employee than to hire and train a new employee with the education background the company is seeking," says Helium. An example of such a circumstance would be to permit a currently employed bookkeeper to work toward an accounting certificate. The bookkeeper would be offered an employee tuition reimbursement for up to $475 per class, per quarter, based on a GPA of 3.0 or higher. There also would be an agreement in place that includes employment of this employee for at least six months after paid-for courses are completed.

In summation, in this age of innovation, there is no one employee-development strategy that fits the needs of every organization. Each company has unique measures for employee-development outcomes. However, in general, it is clear that continuing education for employees has a positive business benefit when compared to the cost.

Entrepreneurs and company leaders should take advantage of the research and development going on in their region and the tremendous array of education and training programs available. These can be the sources of ideas and human capital that will enable them to reinvent their business.

WHAT EMPLOYERS SHOULD DO

What are the implications of innovation and retraining for entrepreneurs and people leading companies in their regions? Following are seven actions entrepreneurs and company leaders should be taking.

- Investing in employee training

- Retaining better employees through tuition-assistance programs

- Urging state governments to invest in continuing education for adults

- Encouraging second-career retired workers

- Allowing time off for continuing education

- Confronting the looming succession crisis

- Changing perceptions about the value of online education

1. Investing in Employee Training

Investment in employee training is rising but is underutilized. According to the University Continuing Education Association, employers continue to increase their investment in employee education, a clear recognition that they need a highly skilled workforce to remain competitive. [176]

2. Promoting Tuition-Assistance Programs

Research conducted by the National Bureau of Economic Research indicates that employees who participate in tuition-assistance programs are less likely to leave their jobs than those who do not participate.[177] Participation in tuition-assistance programs must be promoted at the organization. Unfortunately, only about one in five employees eligible for tuition assistance take advantage of this benefit.

3. Urging States to Invest in Continuing Education for Adults

Organization leaders should urge state policymakers to include adult continuing education in state priorities. Recent trends indicate that higher education in general is receiving reduced support from state legislatures. While student aid from state grant programs has increased greatly in the last fifty years, only a small fraction of that money is available for part-time continuing-education students.

4. Encouraging Second-Career Workers

Organizations should create programs to retrain older workers and provide flexible part-time schedules. According to the AARP, 42 percent of workers age 50 and older would like to work after retiring from their current job, most likely part-time for a new employer.[178]

5. Allowing Time Off for Continuing Education

One roadblock to reskilling is that many employees find it difficult to pursue continuing education while balancing work and family obligations. Employers should offer flexible, convenient educational options to help increase participation.

6. Confronting the Looming Succession Crisis

Due to the impending retirement of millions of baby boomers, many organizations face a looming succession crisis. While retirement has always contributed to employee churn, soon a disproportionate share of employees will become eligible for retirement. Employers need to attack the succession problem with hiring and retention strategies aimed at mature workers, career-changers, and new younger hires. One recruitment incentive offered by the federal government with more frequency is the repayment of student loans.

7. Changing Perceptions About the Value of Online Education

Part of the solution to retrain American workers to be qualified for new technologies is to use new technology in the training. But the lingering attitude that online education lacks the rigor of traditional face-to-face classroom instruction needs to change. Fortunately, the increasing popularity of Web 2.0 tools—including blogs, social media, video sharing, and wikis—is positively influencing how Americans perceive online education.

WELCOME TO THE WORLD OF TWENTY-FIRST-CENTURY INNOVATION

One of the authors of this book was recently in Seattle for meetings on international developments in clean and green technology. Sitting at the breakfast table one morning, it was impossible not to overhear the conversation of six people at the next table, who were in animated discussions about a potential strategic alliance between what sounded like three different enterprises. One was a Web site focused on providing useful and reliable information to pregnant women and mothers of infants and toddlers. The other was a person involved in organic and healthy foods, in particular, healthy baby foods. The third person at the table was someone from a children's-clothing company that has a network of very successful stores across Sweden, a modest online presence, and a desire to link in a very aggressive way with a more robust Web site reaching mothers in the United States.

To begin with, everyone was informally dressed in jeans and short-sleeved shirts. The conversation moved from business statistics and financial figures to personal stories about their own children and feedback from clients about their products. To the casual eavesdropper, it was a cacophony of hard business data, broad-value statements about the importance of natural fabrics in children's clothing, organic foods for children, and market-share percentage growth on a quarterly basis, as well as sales figures and numbers of visitors to Web sites. One of the six was clearly pitching his company, the quality of his team, the high growth of the Web site, and the provision of just-in-time information for moms. Two of the women were pitching why their products are just what moms look for on the Web, based on their sales figures and quarterly growth numbers. Everyone at the table was asking questions and engaging collegially, while occasionally visiting the breakfast buffet. What was clearly going on was the development of a strategic alliance between complementary Web sites and products from a group of young entrepreneurs—two women, four men—all of whom were committed to promoting a healthy lifestyle and healthy products for young mothers, infants, and toddlers.

The principals in this conversation were not in a boardroom with PowerPoint slides, sharing pages and pages of charts embedded in a slick business plan that was being discussed by MBAs in dress-for-success suits. They were eating and chatting about personal things, including things such as they grew up and what values were important to them. Over and over again, our coauthor heard the comment, "It's not just about our products; it's about a way of life." The Web provider and the product providers engaged in this discussion are, in fact, known entities in both the United States and Sweden, looking to further extend their reach in order to serve the values of people concerned about environmental products and healthy food. They are also looking to turn what are now hundred-million-dollar businesses into billion-dollar businesses—four men and two women doing business the twenty-first-century way. Welcome to the new global economy!

THE GOOD NEWS FOR AMERICA

The good news is that the American Dream of good jobs for all is alive and well. This only holds true, however, if collectively, as a nation, organizationally, as companies and employers, and individually as members of America's dynamic workforce, we engage some critical realities. What we have attempted to do in this book is introduce these critical realities and suggest some very specific strategies by drawing on the story of San Diego's interesting economic transformation, as well as trends in the American workforce.

We have argued that the challenge today is two-sided. It involves the need to support companies that create jobs through innovation and entrepreneurship. Equally important is the need to better align the innovation and job-creation systems with workforce education and training. In this way we can minimize the need to import workers or export jobs, in order to realize the promise of innovative new technologies.

The critical realities we have discussed throughout this book can be summed up in terms of five broad assumptions about what can assure that the American workforce benefits from the innovation economy, moving forward. If individuals cannot accept these new realities, if organizations are unwilling to adjust to these new realities, and, if our public policy is unable to shift focus and enable strategic investments, moving forward, our competitiveness will be at risk.

So, in conclusion, we say to our reader, These are the critical realities to keep in mind as you think about what it will take to close America's job gap:

Change. Rapid changes in technology are transforming the content of everything we use and everything we do on a daily basis. Combine this with globalization of both producers and consumers of products, and it means that uncertainty about who will dominate which technologies and markets is very high. But it also means that the opportunity to develop new technologies and products that reach new and important markets is also very high. But nothing is certain; change is the name of the game for all economies and for all individuals.

Small Systems. As we pointed out in Section One, large systems and large companies move at a slower pace, in part because they are overburdened by long-term investments in equipment, people, and distribution systems that may not be suited to the new technology and emerging market opportunities. Small companies tend to take bigger risks and can be formed and disassembled more quickly. More important, small companies enable highly adaptive behavior because of fewer layers of bureaucracy and fewer overhead burdens. In short, they can be nimble. However, the jobs they are currently creating are not enough to keep Americans employed. We need to invest in many more small, innovative companies as well as the technologies on which they are based and the entrepreneurs who enable the realization of these technologies in the marketplace. This is how we can increase the job-creation process in this country.

Regionalism. Given the importance of the first two factors we have identified, the reality is that it is at the regional level that the research and development is done, the companies get started, and jobs are quickly created and expanded. It's a matter of scale. Innovation and job creation require the ability to quickly mobilize stakeholders and competencies. This way, an enterprise can adapt as circumstances change and mount production, marketing, and distribution channels quickly with people who are ready to move into the jobs these opportunities create. Regional platforms, as research demonstrates, have been very effective launching pads for global companies as well as for the sustainability of regional prosperity.

Collaboration and Inclusiveness. With great uncertainty and high levels of complexity, what regions need is lots of collaborative and inclusive organizations and agencies that are supporting small-business development, the work of basic researchers, the applications of new technology, and the formation of new small businesses. This is especially true for complex entrepreneurial technology enterprises that require a wide range of business and professional stakeholders and get launched with high levels of uncertainty about their success. By building inclusive collaborative platforms, of which CONNECT of San Diego is but one example, it is possible for regions to create successful companies and good jobs quickly and continuously.

All Work is Learning. None of the above can benefit the American workforce, unless we renew our commitment to learning as a critical component of all work. The "one job, one set of skills for a lifetime" mentality is a recipe for failure. Whether one is a welder, a neuroscientist, a gynecologist, a structural engineer, or a cabinet-maker, science and technology is changing the content of the materials and processes involved in the work that is being done. Globalization is affecting the market opportunities as well as the potential competitors and partners in doing that work. It is critical that, regardless of their skill level, workers are allowed to take advantage of opportunities to learn new things continuously. Through continuous learning, workers' skills remain competitive and their capacity to earn good wages is sustainable.

It is not clear if we, as a nation—as American employers and American workers—are prepared to engage these critical realities. The crisis in the American economy over the last few years suggests we are still trying to find our way back to prosperity. Our hope is that the ideas and insights provided in this book will contribute, in some small way, to that return to prosperity.

FINAL THOUGHTS

America has a long and impressive history of innovation, entrepreneurship, and company creation. We must continue to reinforce this unique quality through public policies and strategic investments that enable research, investment in risky ventures, and support for entrepreneurs and business creators. However, in this new age of global competitiveness where the beneficiaries of innovation, in terms of workforce, can be anywhere in the world, we must transform the lagging American workforce-development system into the kind of world-class system we already have in place for innovation and entrepreneurship. That means, first and foremost, aligning our workforce-development strategies with our innovation-development strategies by building new kinds of partnerships between the regional drivers of innovation and regional providers of education and training. This can only happen if we, as Americans, come to grips with the fact that our future depends on the adaptability and educability of each of us to the new realities of global markets and global competitiveness.

For those readers who desire a deeper look into innovation and job creation, the following addendum provides the story behind the story of America's job gap. Companies that want to grow, workers looking for growing sectors, and policymakers who want to fuel economic growth have much to gain by understanding the dynamics of the innovation age. Part 1 examines America's unique culture of innovation. Part 2 is a breakdown of innovation ecosystems. Part 3 is an in-depth overview of the San Diego innovation ecosystem.

The role innovation can play in job retention and creation is dramatically demonstrated in San Diego's experience, a region where median income has increased while across the country, median income has declined. The San Diego lesson is this: Any region serious about innovation and job creation should strive to create platforms that regularly bring together the four key players: the research community, the entrepreneurs and investors, the economic developers, and the educators and workforce-training organizations. This is the best way to support the innovative companies that create good jobs and to aid workers looking for rewarding careers in the age of innovation.

ADDENDUM:

DEEPER REFLECTIONS
ON INNOVATION AND JOB CREATION

PART 1

America's Unique Culture of Innovation

The United States has the most powerful economy in the world; however, this cannot be sustained unless we begin to think deeply and strategically about innovation. Innovation is embedded in America's DNA. Most of us feel strongly that our culture and heritage are conducive to innovation in light of our pioneering spirit, individual creativity, entrepreneurial economy, work ethic, and our society that has attracted the best and the brightest to our shores from all over the world. Innovation, along with entrepreneurship, has been the heart of America's economic growth and its capacity to create and grow good jobs throughout the last century.

> "To a considerable extent, scientists and innovators have shaped our nation. Americans have always excelled in basic science."

Between the late nineteenth century and the end of the twentieth century, the United States had little trouble establishing and maintaining its place as the world's leader in science and technology. To a considerable extent, scientists and innovators have shaped our nation. Americans have always excelled in basic science. The long list of Nobel Prize winners over the past five decades is a testimony to that. But America has also excelled in applied science—improving upon ideas already in existence and commercializing those ideas into products for which there are significant markets.

Thomas Edison did not invent the lightbulb, but he made it workable.

Samuel Morse did not invent the telegraph, but he made it practical. Many had tried to achieve powered flight before the Wright brothers conquered gravity in a controlled flight at Kitty Hawk in 1903. These people were actually tinkerers of the highest order—innovators with great interest in and commitment to the hands-on work that transforms ideas into realities.[179] When ideas become translated into realities, they create wealth and good jobs, both of which benefit the national good.

This country's culture of innovation has been fundamental to its prosperity, and the list of American innovation successes is long, impressive, and varied. For instance, in 2009, four of the eight winners of the *Economist* magazine's innovation awards were Americans. They include Jimmy Wales for Wikipedia, the free online encyclopedia; Steve Chen and Chad Hurley for YouTube, the popular video-sharing Web site; Arthur Rosenfeld for the promotion of energy-efficiency; and Bill and Melinda Gates for developing a businesslike approach to philanthropy (their foundation provides an enabling platform for nonprofit organizations that are improving the lives of millions of people around the world).

As a nation we have always risen to the challenge of difficult times. A large number of our stellar companies have been recession-era start-ups, including companies known for their commitment to innovation, such as: IBM, Disney, General Electric, HP, Kraft, Microsoft, McDonalds, Hyatt Hotels, FedEx, CNN, MTV Networks, Trader Joe's, *Sports Illustrated*, Electronic Arts, and Google.[180]

Why is innovation so important? It raises productivity, and that translates into higher profits, higher wages, and higher incomes. It also gives rise to new businesses and new product lines in existing companies, and that translates into much-needed new jobs.[181]

RENEWING THE SPIRIT OF INNOVATION

Despite our remarkable history of creativity, invention, and innovation, the recent economic recession has taken the wind from our sails. America is fast becoming a nation of pessimists. It does not have to be that way; this is not who we are as Americans.

Let us not forget that recessions are not new. We have been here many times, and each time, the United States has come back more prosperous. It may be surprising to know that since 1945 America has experienced thirteen economic downturns with an average duration of ten months. Unfortunately, the recent recession—the Great Recession of 2008–2009—has been the longest and most painful in terms of job losses in the post–World War II period. We are recovering, but it will be uneven and a slower process than what we have experienced in the past.

We need to shore up our economy and firm up our economic future by creating more sustainable twenty-first-century jobs beyond those generated by the federal stimulus program. Business as usual will not do it. "Innovation and Entrepreneurship" must be the new mantra for our economic policy, if we are to regain our economic well-being and maintain our global competitiveness. Distinguished journalists such as Thomas Friedman and economists such as Paul Krugman have been especially assertive about this necessity. Having weathered the destabilizing financial crisis, America is beginning to see a renewed focus on the power of innovation and entrepreneurial enterprises as a major path to prosperity.

Business creation, driven by innovation, is the best and, perhaps, only way for America to create meaningful and sustainable jobs that will be the foundation of our future prosperity. Instead of simply creating new waves of the same old consumer products and services that continue to exacerbate our social and environmental problems, we need to focus on transforming smart ideas that address real needs into valuable products and services with a worldwide market.

"Innovation and Entrepreneurship"— We need to repeat this frequently and practice it consistently until it rekindles the sparks of imagination and creativity that have been part of our national psyche and culture for over two centuries. A new "Sputnik moment" has arrived and there is great urgency. The spirit of innovation is deeply rooted in our culture, but we often smother it with a cloak of complacency worn by those who don't believe America could rank less than Number 1 and, therefore, need not make any efforts to stay on top. Well, America is losing its place to less-complacent countries and, if we are to maintain our position as a global economic leader, we cannot neglect the critical need to encourage and support our innovators and entrepreneurs.

For the United States to prosper in the twenty-first century, our nation must encourage the growth of world-class innovation regions throughout the country. The good news is that we already have a number of excellent models, including the iconic Silicon Valley; the Route 128 region around Boston; North Carolina's Research Triangle; the high-tech region of greater Austin, Texas; and the innovation region of California's southernmost city, San Diego. From the latter, we can learn a great deal about regional economic transformation, as a result of building innovative clusters of globally competitive start-up and high-growth companies that create thousands of good jobs.

PART 2

The Innovation Ecosystem

The most effective framework for understanding innovation is to imagine an ecosystem—an innovation ecosystem. Looking at an economy from a more organic, less mechanical perspective has been gaining popularity among economists. William Wulf, the researcher, entrepreneur, and former president of the National Academy of Engineering, has used the phrase "ecology of innovation" to describe how various factors interact in an economy to enhance or hinder its ability to innovate. These factors, according to Wulf, include intellectual-property law, tax codes, patent procedures, export controls, and immigration regulations. Together they represent a high-tech innovation ecosystem. Added to this is emerging research on the importance of social networks, intermediary organizations, and a culture that supports risk-taking and learns from failure rather than punishes failure.[182]

> **"Like every living ecosystem, survival is the outcome of the complex interplay of a number of factors."**

Like every living ecosystem, survival is the outcome of the complex interplay of a number of factors. An innovation ecosystem is a dynamic, adaptive organism that creates, consumes, and transforms knowledge and ideas into streams of innovative products and services through the continuous formation of new companies, within a complex matrix of relationships among various stakeholders in the region (see Figure 17).

Figure 17
Key Elements of Innovation Ecosystems

The unifying forces among all these pieces are:

- Alignment of resources and capabilities so all the components of the system are moving in the same direction and ready to deploy.

- A community characterized by adaptive learning companies and services that collaborate in order to compete.

- A diverse array of formal and informal networks, intermediaries, and integrators.

James F. Moore formally introduced the concept of a business ecosystem in a *Harvard Business Review* article in 1993.[183] He described a business ecosystem as:

[An] economic community supported by a foundation of interacting organizations and individuals—the organisms of the business world. This economic community produces goods and services of value to customers, who are themselves members of the ecosystem. The member organizations also include suppliers, lead producers, competitors, and other stakehold-ers. Over time, they co-evolve their capabilities and roles, and tend to align themselves with the directions set by one or more central companies. Those companies holding leadership roles may change over time, but the func-tion of an ecosystem leader is valued by the community because it enables members to move toward shared visions to align their investments and to find mutually supportive roles.

This ecosystem of high-value-added industries also requires a contin-uous infusion of both technically skilled and formally educated workers in order to design, commercialize, manufacture, and service new products on an expanding scale. Thus, it creates a wide variety of good jobs. Major companies such as Hewlett Packard, IBM, SAP, Microsoft, Softbank, and Intel initially used this economic community concept for business-strat-egy development. Lately, it has been more broadly applied to many prob-lems, including foreign policy, as well as economic-development strategy development.

So what are the fundamental elements that serve and sustain an in-novation economy successfully over decades? We are suggesting eight key elements that include: 1. Research Infrastructure, 2. Entrepreneurs, 3. Investment Capital, 4. Ready Workforce, 5. Business Environment, 6. Quality of Life, 7. Social and Professional Networks, 8. Intermediary and Integrative Organizations.

INNOVATION IN AN INTERACTIVE WEB OF THE ECOSYSTEM

As in any biological ecosystem, these key elements work in concert; no one element stands on its own. And, just like in nature, these elements form a web of relationships that constantly nurture and interact with one another in synergistic ways that strengthen the overall economic environ-ment and contribute to the resilience and sustainability of innovation hubs. While one or two elements—research institutions and entrepreneurs, for example—are key factors in maintaining the balance of the system, elements such as the talent pool of scientific, technical, and support services; quality of life; and business environment are also critical. Venture capitalists choose where they live and work and appreciate a region with cultural and recreational assets; they have neither the need nor the desire to compromise their tastes. A research university may be outstanding in training engineers and scientists, but if a region's business environment or culture does not encourage entrepreneurship, talented innovators may relocate to more supportive areas such as Silicon Valley or Austin, Texas.

As we will see, some or all of these same elements can be found in many regions, but the density, quality, and richness of these elements in regions such as Seattle and San Diego are the sources of their sustained economic vitality. For example, other regions of the country have an abundance of skilled workers (e.g., Detroit), but, for various reasons, the industries that employ them—such as the auto industry—and the surrounding social environment have not enabled a culture of innovation that emphasizes lifelong learning, creativity, risk-taking, and openness to new ideas. Neither have they encouraged the kind of adaptability that is critical in an innovation workforce.

Other regions (e.g., Spain) may have an abundance of entrepreneurs, but they may approach starting a business as a "lifestyle business" rather than taking the more aggressive "start, grow, sell" path of the serial entrepreneur, especially in the high value-added tech sector. Serial entrepreneurs are catalysts and active agents in the social and professional networks that inspire and support new entrepreneurs, thus fueling the innovation economy. Without them, a region's networks lack the vitality to stimulate and support world-class business leaders. In the following paragraphs, we take a look at each of these key elements individually.[184]

Key Element 1: Research Universities

An innovation ecosystem needs at least one, if not several, primary sources of intellectual property, the essence of innovation. Research universities, think tanks, and corporate labs provide discoveries and new technologies capable of providing new solutions or adaptation of existing solutions—ideas with innovation potential. They also provide critical training for an essential part of the region's workforce and offer companies access to high-tech labs and equipment. Technology-transfer programs help facilitate the commercialization of IP in a region, particularly if they are well integrated in a vibrant innovation ecosystem.

World-class research universities such as UC San Diego, and research centers such as M.D. Anderson in Houston and the Donald Danforth Plant Science Center in St. Louis, form the foundation of a world-class innovation economy in many ways: via the generation and licensing of intellectual property; through the involvement of faculty as consultants and advisers to businesses; by supporting faculty in capitalizing on their innovations; by providing the private sector with a steady supply of talented engineers, designers, managers, etc.; by providing innovators with access to cutting-edge laboratories and equipment; and by encouraging a continuous dialogue among industry experts, faculty, and students.

Research institutions play a pivotal role in the evolution and success of innovation economies. The research they do is wide-ranging and incredibly regionally relevant. One need only point to UC Davis's ecology-research contributions to the wine industry in the Napa Valley; The University of Texas at Austin's petro-chemical research contributions to the oil and gas industry of the state; MIT's role in making the Boston region a global hub for information and computer technologies. When knowledge and innovation are the primary drivers of economic growth and transformation, world-class centers of knowledge, discovery, and development represent invaluable economic assets. San Diego, the subject of Section Two, continues to flourish, primarily, because the region is home to an outstanding world-class research university: UC San Diego, as well as fifty free-standing research institutes, such as the Salk Institute for Biological Studies, which collectively attract close to $2 billion annually in research funding.

Key Element 2: Entrepreneurs

In the innovation ecosystem, the entrepreneur is the biological host. Without the unique talents, traits, and tenacity of the entrepreneur, bold, new ideas would never see the light of day. We all have lots of new ideas, but the entrepreneur, driven by the energy and excitement of the core idea that is the seed of innovation, as well as by a hefty dose of self-interest and visions of personal gain, makes the commitment and takes the risk to manifest the innovation as a new product or service. A culture of entrepreneurship and a tradition of serial entrepreneurship are key features of successful ecosystems.

Entrepreneurs turn ideas into products. Their willingness and ability to accept the risks associated with taking an innovative product to market can be enabled or frustrated by a region's culture. Any region striving to develop a sustainable innovation economy needs to foster a culture of entrepreneurship in its business community and nurture next-generation entrepreneurs in its educational institutions.

An entrepreneur is typically a problem-solver, a dreamer, even a visionary—someone who likes to achieve the supposedly unachievable and solve a problem that seems to defy solution. A deep belief in the product around which an idea is formed, and the willingness and determination to bring that product to market, are the hallmarks of successful entrepreneurs. Quite often, entrepreneurs take significant personal risks and assume tremendous financial burdens. While entrepreneurs often turn to angel investors (many of whom are successful entrepreneurs themselves) or venture-capital firms for money, entrepreneurs inherently have "skin in the game," meaning personal investments, as they strive to bring concepts to life as technologies or products. It is important to distinguish between lifestyle entrepreneurs (small family businesses), traditional entrepreneurs (limited-growth companies), and tech entrepreneurs (high-cost tech and talent companies). The tech entrepreneurs require a level of technical know-how vis-à-vis global product standards and markets, capital infusions, and levels of talent on the team, which require a very different range of skills than those of the lone entrepreneur starting a family business, a local/regional service, or a manufacturing enterprise.

Entrepreneurs, especially in high-tech, require a highly entrepreneurial and risk-taking environment with a strong work ethic, where bold moves, radical thinking, and even the occasional honest failure are marks of distinction. Communities with an abundance of these types of entrepreneurs, such as Seattle or San Diego, have this culture.[185] Most images of entrepreneurs are of a person who is highly individualistic, even "pig-headed," blessed with brilliant ideas, endowed with talent, who takes decisive actions against all odds that result in success. In reality, however, the technology entrepreneur is quite different because the problems he/she is attacking are of an order of complexity requiring multiple forms of knowledge, competence, and experience. The Entrepreneurship Center at the University of Ohio offers this profile of a typical high-tech entrepreneur:[186]

- Revolutionary: wants to change the world with great ideas and new technologies

- Wants to be a global player from the start

- Expert at developing an extensive local network

- Highly competitive and a risk-taker

- Believes in speed—time to market is critical

- Wants great financial reward but also seeks respect, influence, and fame

- Ultimately wants to control the market and not just the company

- Team player in the organization and the network

- Loves to celebrate and recognize achievements and success of others

- May become an angel investor to repeat success and share expertise and ideas

Contrary to the notion that the typical entrepreneur is a workaholic loner, the successful entrepreneur is someone who is connected.[187] Building a new business in the fast-moving technology world is rarely a Lone Ranger task. While successful entrepreneurs are often engaged in long hours of hard work, their most valuable work involves building an extensive network of managers, colleagues, investors, suppliers, and potential customers with whom they actively share ideas, business strategies, knowledge and experience, and comments and critiques. This is why supportive, intermediary organizations play such a critical role in successful high-tech regions. The social and professional networks are especially important for entrepreneurs. They link inventors, engineers, entrepreneurs, investors, and business professionals together, support the pre-transactional trust development described earlier, enable building the teams, and offer access to the diverse forms of expertise critical to starting and growing successful technology companies.

Technology clusters that grow and evolve also typically benefit from the contribution of serial entrepreneurs. A serial entrepreneur is someone who enjoys the process of starting, growing, and selling a business (hopefully, at a profit), then starting and growing a new business—sometimes in a totally unrelated field. Serial entrepreneurs also invest personal money and time, as well as their connections to resources and market in new and emerging companies, usually in their region.

Not all entrepreneurs are successful, nor is every successful entrepreneur going to be successful the second, third, or fourth time around. Resilient innovation economies are rooted in the indomitable spirit and persistence of entrepreneurs who want to change the world with their ideas, despite the risks and hard work involved, and who are able to work with others to achieve this end. These entrepreneurs rarely stop with one company, but engage multiple times and often in multiple ways with new ventures. Dr. Bill Musgrave, president and CEO of the Enterprise Network of Silicon Valley, says "No one cares about who you are—your title, how much money you have, or the color of your skin. What counts in the region is what you can achieve. It is the best place, bar none, for entrepreneurs to launch their dreams."

Key Element 3: Investment Capital

Ideas and solutions are the soul of innovation. Money is the lifeblood. Access to seed and early-stage money from angel investors during the start-up stages, and money for expansion from venture capital firms is critical for high-tech companies. Access to pro bono services, free or low-cost space and facilities, and innovative lending practices also enable putting together financially viable start-up enterprises. Investors support innovation by providing entrepreneurs with more than money; they also provide valuable business expertise, links to personal contacts, and access to social and professional networks.

Very few high-tech ventures can launch and grow to become world-class companies without large infusions of cash at crucial stages of development. Innovation ecosystems require convenient access to high net-worth individuals (sometimes called angel investors), multimillion-dollar venture-capital firms, and top investment banks. The brutal competition for cash is one of the primary survival tests for both innovations and entrepreneurs. Theoretically, this competitive process should assure that only the best innovations make it to the market, but, as we have seen, this has not always proven to be true. Investors do more than just provide money; they also offer a wealth of technical expertise, business experience, and valuable connections to resources and important people.

Typical high-tech entrepreneurs are not interested in lifestyle businesses—firms that merely support a certain lifestyle for them and their families. Rather, they have an ambitious vision that usually involves bringing a revolutionary new product to the market, a dream of reaching global markets, and, certainly, making lots of money by doing so. As a result, they are prepared to share equity/ownership of their enterprise because a small percentage of a big "hit," i.e., a $50–$500-million company, represents a larger return than 100 percent of a $5–$10-million company.

It's a rare high-tech company that can scale big enough and fast enough without an infusion of cash. Cash is the lifeblood of high-tech companies, particularly when a company is likely to be engaged in months or years of product development, during which there will be little or no income generated by sales. Like the vision itself, the entrepreneur's need for cash usually is quite large and runs into millions of dollars. The ability of an entrepreneur to raise sufficient capital to pursue his/her vision is often as important as the ability to envision and invent a new product or service.

When we think of cash needs on this scale, we often think of venture capital (VC), but in reality, it is a rare venture that actually gets funded by a VC firm—at least initially. More often than not, entrepreneurs invest considerable personal resources (both cash and sweat equity) before they seek additional funds. It's not uncommon for entrepreneurs to take out a second mortgage on their homes and "max out" their credit cards in the early stages of launching a company. And many companies start out "bootstrapping" (providing customers consulting services or selling a single product) while they are developing more innovative technologies or applications.

The presence of large and more media-visible venture-capital firms has often overshadowed the role of angel investors in the development of start-up companies, especially in the high-tech innovation economy. VC investments are typically in the millions of dollars and frequently attract press coverage, while angel investments are typically smaller and occur in more informal ways. Angel investors are the largest source of seed and start-up capital. Along with government programs such as SBIR and SBA, they provide the early-stage funding before VC steps in. The University of New Hampshire's Center for Venture Research reports that "angels continue to be the largest source of seed and start-up capital, with 46 percent of 2006 angel investments in the seed and start-up stage. This preference for seed and start-up investing is followed closely by post–seed/start-up investments of 40 percent." In a 2000 study, MIT's Entrepreneurship Center categorized angel investors in four primary groups:

- Guardian Angels, who bring both entrepreneurial and industry expertise. Many have been successful entrepreneurs in the same sector as the new companies they support.

- Entrepreneur Angels, who have experience starting companies but come from different industry sectors.

- Operational Angels, who bring industry experience and expertise, but, generally, from large, established companies, and may lack first-hand experience with the travails of a start-up.

- Financial Angels, who typically invest purely for the financial return.

A 2004 survey by the University of New Hampshire's Center for Venture Research found that the typical angel investor has the following characteristics:

- Middle-aged and male: Over 90 percent are male and between 40 and 60 years old.

- Holds a master's degree or other advanced degree and has prior start-up experience

- Has an annual income in the $100,000–$250,000 range

- Invests 2.5 times a year at roughly $25,000–$50,000 per deal ($130,000 total)

- Seldom invests in more than 10 percent of a deal

- Seeks 20 percent compounded per-annum returns

- Expects to hold an investment for five to seven years

- Likes to invest in the technology he knows and prefers manufacturing and product companies

- Prefers to invest in fast-growing start-ups, and often prefers to take an active consulting or advisor position with a company

- Likes to invest with others and prefers to invest close by (typically, within fifty to three hundred miles from home)

- Invests to receive a high rate of return (e.g., 20 percent to 30 percent internal rate of return)

- Learns about deals from friends, 30 percent from accountants or attorneys

- Would like to see more deals, and refers deals to other private investors[188]

While seed- and early-stage investments by angels are often critical for launch, angels are rarely able to provide funding sufficient to take companies to the next level and beyond. This is the role that venture-capital (VC) firms play. While the typical angel investment today is under $250,000 and, even when syndicated, rarely reaches beyond a couple million dollars, the average VC deal in the second quarter of 2009 in a place such as San Diego was $5 million plus. As one venture capitalist put it, it takes almost as much time and effort to find, screen, and close a smaller angel deal as it does a large VC deal. As defined by the National Venture Capital Association, venture-capital firms are "pools of capital, typically organized as a limited partnership, that invest in companies that represent the opportunity for a high rate of return within five to seven years. Far from being simply passive financiers, venture capitalists foster growth in companies through their involvement in the management, strategic marketing, and planning of their investee companies. They are entrepreneurs first and financiers second."[189]

Key Element 4: Workforce

No business venture can thrive without a skilled and dedicated workforce. Vibrant innovation communities are magnets for talent from all over the world, and the diversity of these regions' workforce has been a source of their strength and success. More so even than the social environment, the region's business environment is a melting pot of people and ideas from a wide range of ethnic backgrounds, academic disciplines, business cultures, etc. At the same time, as in every ecosystem, organisms (i.e., skilled workers) at every level are opportunistic. In a culture where job-hopping is an accepted practice, retaining talented employees is challenging for every company. As a result, companies are constantly experimenting with various innovations in the workplace to keep their employees loyal and happy.

An innovation ecosystem needs a large pool of talented workers to fill the myriad of positions created by new start-ups, expanding companies, and well-established firms. Workforce diversity brings new ideas, new connections, and access to global resources. Smart companies understand that competition for talented workers is stiff and that perks are often an important factor in keeping employees happy and loyal.

Even more important, companies and communities that are serious about growing profitable and sustainable high-tech enterprises and clusters of enterprises invest in developing, recruiting, retaining, and continuously reeducating the talent pool they need. It is impossible to achieve significant gains in profitability and regional prosperity without having a workforce capable of deploying new technologies and building high-growth enterprises. Section One of this book describes the wide array of talent—from semi-skilled to highly skilled, from university-educated to Ph.D.- and postdoctoral-level talent—in an innovation economy. There is a significant interdependence between innovation companies and the talent pool they can tap into. That is why in successful regions you find local colleges and universities and, on occasion, workforce-development agencies, in frequent and deep conversation with the R&D community and the leaders of start-up and growth companies. In this manner, the education and training organizations are able to stay abreast of where technology is going and how it is affecting existing jobs or creating potentially whole-new industries with new skill requirements. This social dynamic has to be in place for a region to not only produce important inventions and occasional breakthrough products, but to have the ability to commercialize those products and build businesses and create wealth, as well as create jobs locally.

Just as money is the key fuel for innovative ventures, knowledge and information are vital for survival and success, particularly when competing on a global scale. In a rapidly changing global marketplace where transformative technologies emerge at an ever-increasing speed, information is critical and takes many forms. Information comes from a myriad of sources, especially formal and informal social and professional networks. Information, ideas, contacts, and connections flow freely despite the hypercompetitive spirit that pervades the region. When working on products and ventures characterized by high-risk and uncertain outcomes, pre-transactional bonds of familiarity and trust are also essential. Uncertain ventures require nimbleness and adaptability, as well as personal flexibility. It is essential to build a start-up team with the technical and business know-how and the chemistry to be able to track progress and make midcourse corrections and hard choices in order to reach the final goal and profitability. Dense social networks enable the development of trust, as well as shared knowledge. The degree to which a business community has successfully developed these pre-transactional networks and managed the tension between collegiality and competitiveness has proven to be a major contributor to the unique culture of entrepreneurial business environments that create innovative, high-value-added companies and jobs.

Key Element 5: Social and Professional Networks

Just as money is the key fuel for innovative ventures, knowledge and information are vital for survival and success, particularly when competing on a global scale. In a rapidly changing global marketplace where transformative technologies emerge at an ever-increasing speed, information is critical and takes many forms. Information comes from a myriad of sources, especially formal and informal social and professional networks. Ideas, contacts, and connections flow freely despite the hypercompetitive spirit that pervades the region. When working on products and ventures characterized by high-risk and uncertain outcomes, pre-transactional bonds of familiarity and trust are also essential. Uncertain ventures require nimbleness and adaptability, as well as personal flexibility. It is essential to build a start-up team with the technical and business know-how and the chemistry to be able to track progress and make midcourse corrections and hard choices in order to reach the final goal and profitability. Dense social networks enable the development of trust, as well as shared knowledge. The degree to which a business community has successfully developed these pre-transactional networks and managed the tension between collegiality and competitiveness has proven to be a major contributor to the unique culture of entrepreneurial business environments that create innovative high-value-added companies and jobs.

The importance of social and professional networks cannot be overstated in any discussion of regions with a successful record of innovation, company formation, cluster development, and ultimately, job creation—in particular, high-wage job creation. The social dynamics are radically different than one finds in older, more traditional locales with legacy industries from the nineteenth to mid-twentieth centuries. Such communities have a tendency to be much more hierarchical and reliant on established institutions, including a local power structure that is often dominated by leadership in specific industries and, frequently, old families and/or a long tradition of organized labor and civic interests. Research on such regions suggests that it is harder for ideas to percolate from the bottom up and that the collaborative structures that produce the kind of boundary-spanning, cross-functional networking that is so nurturing of creative and innovative enterprises are in short supply.[190]

In contrast, the culture and social dynamics of innovation regions tend to be nonhierarchical and characterized by multiple centers of leadership gravity. Management style within organizations, as well as leadership style in the community, is built around consultative, inclusive activities and shared responsibility. And, finally, in the absence of legacy industries and old families and old forms of philanthropy that more traditional communities often look to for leadership, there is a more bottom-up approach. One finds higher levels of individual participation and even personal and small-company contributions of cash and resources into activities, which promise to help grow the regional economy in dynamic, innovative environments. Innovative communities value traditional credentials less than they do outcomes, products, and achievements. As a consequence, they are able to quickly integrate highly diverse forms of talent and newcomers with talent or a record of success. It takes much longer for "outsiders" to become "insiders" in more conventional communities dominated by more traditional industrial histories.

When one looks at the growth of the technology clusters in locales such as Seattle; San Diego; Austin, Texas; and the Research Triangle Park in North Carolina over the last twenty-five years, what one sees are communities that have been characterized by high rates of immigration of diverse populations, most of whom are seeking to create new kinds of institutions and new kinds of companies. They have encountered few local barriers to those aspirations. In contrast, cities such as Detroit, St. Louis, and Pittsburgh, until very recently, were less welcoming to such individuals and these sorts of high-risk enterprises.

Key Element 6: Business Environment

A region's business environment affects corporate viability and the ability of the region to compete in the global marketplace. It also affects the fundamental ecology of innovation in the region. Without favorable business conditions, including adequate professional and business services (e.g., IP attorneys, financing specialists), companies operate at a competitive disadvantage and the relationships that exist between the various components of the ecology are out of balance.

In a natural environment—just as latitude, temperature, moisture, air pressure, topography, and many other factors cause the weather of a region to be in constant flux—a myriad of interacting factors in an economic ecosystem is continuously changing. At any given time, the business climate represents a snapshot of the overall business and economic environment at that time. In addition to macro factors (e.g., the social framework and political structure, physical and economic infrastructures, population profile, etc.), a region's day-to-day business climate is influenced by other constantly changing factors. Among these are the prevailing attitudes of the local, regional, and state governments, as well as those of the financial institutions, toward business and economic activity, the current taxation regimen, costs of living, and so forth. In addition, the presence of various business services such as appropriate types of accounting and legal firms, banking, and various types of consultancies is critical.

Key Element 7: Quality of Life

As discussed earlier, quality of life affects all these cultural and social dynamics. Innovators, entrepreneurs, investors, engineers, and the many others who contribute to the success of a company, all appreciate and often demand a high quality of life for themselves and their families. Good schools and easy access to recreational opportunities and cultural venues are important factors for defining the quality of life in a region. The importance of quality of life is not to be overlooked; it ranks as a key element of a region's innovation ecosystem. Its importance does not supersede the chance to do innovative work or grow and maintain a cultural and business environment that supports entrepreneurship in initially attracting inventors, entrepreneurs, and start-up business talent. It does, however, contribute to a region's ability to retain the sort of talent that ultimately contributes to growing regional innovation clusters and high-wage jobs.

Location matters, even in the footloose digital age. It matters a great deal because knowledge workers are a fairly sophisticated bunch. They value access to universities as well as quality schools for their kids. They appreciate cultural richness and civic virtue. They expect choice in housing and transportation, diversity of employment opportunities, a good physical environment, good food, and good coffee (an important fuel for the innovation economy).

A culturally and aesthetically rich city like Seattle, Boston, or San Diego becomes a catalyst and agent of economic vitality for the entire region. This can be easily observed via the growth of art organizations, entertainment, and upscale shopping and restaurant linkages, as well as philanthropy in these hubs of innovation and job creation.

Key Element 8: Intermediary and Integrative Organizations

As noted above, rapid knowledge flows; high levels of trust; and a capacity to mobilize the expertise, skill, and know-how needed to develop a product and launch a successful business are greatly enabled by pretransactional relationships forged in groups and activities. Communities with a rich and varied array of boundary-spanning, cross-professional networks seem to be more effective at supporting innovation than siloed ones. These intermediary organizations not only facilitate relationships, but represent a community of experience, know-how, connections to expertise, and access to resources that can be mobilized as companies start up and navigate the ups and downs of becoming a bona fide business with customers and revenues. Research indicates that where such intermediaries exist, more entrepreneurial enterprises succeed and more jobs are created. The CONNECT organization in San Diego, a nonprofit innovation accelerator, is a prime example.

PART 3

How San Diego Retained and Created High-Value Jobs

The role innovation can play in job retention and creation is dramatically demonstrated in the experience of the San Diego region where, in the last ten years, the median income increased by 4.3 percent while across the country it dropped by 4.1 percent. The challenge in an economy increasingly driven by invention and innovation is that products and processes continuously change at ever-increasing rates. These products and services include health and medical treatments and preventatives; cell phones and computers; and how clothing is designed, manufactured, and distributed. That is why Peter Drucker, the management guru, said more than thirty years ago "All work is learning."

> **"One of the dilemmas in America today is that too many people are clinging to the vanishing job for which they were initially trained or educated."**

Regrettably, many still think that learning precedes work, i.e., "the big thing is getting the job, and the rest is just doing the job." The problem with this line of thinking is that the job is constantly changing, and the knowledge and skill requirements it had when you started the job are no longer sufficient to accomplish the outcomes for which you are being paid. Often the job disappears, replaced by new and, in many cases, more-efficient technologies. In the '50s and '60s, women were flooding the workforce as telephone operators and bank tellers; but by the '70s and '80s, cellular phones and ATMs emerged, and their training became irrelevant. In the '60s, ailments involving treating internal diseases required spending days in the hospital after major "knock-the-patient-out" surgeries. Today, angiograms, laparoscopic surgeries, and orthopaedic procedures involve different tools and different kinds of skills in health-care workers. As recently as in the '90s, large city newspapers and network television dominated the communications landscape, whereas today, fragmentation across multiple media and expanding uses of the Internet mean the jobs of printers, advertisers, journalists, and editors have been transformed.

Finally, new jobs are created—jobs for which there are no established rules related to how to perform tasks, no established credentials, and no agreed-upon standards. Such jobs emerge from the doing of the work and eventually become more structured and defined, enabling more standardized forms of education, training, and certification. But these new jobs, too, keep changing over time and eventually disappear.

One of the dilemmas in America today is that too many people are clinging to the vanishing job for which they were initially trained or educated. They don't want their job to change—much less diminish in importance or disappear entirely. People want certainty when the realities of modern life are change and uncertainty that require constant adaptability not only in how we do things, but in the things we do in our daily work. An economy cannot survive, much less thrive, if its citizens refuse to update, retrain, even completely refocus their skills for the work that is available and needs to be done because of changing economic imperatives. San Diego has been unusually (albeit, imperfectly) adept at embracing these imperatives, while many communities across America, especially those in the industrial heartland, have lagged. Workers and management alike have been waiting for their old jobs to return and resisting the requirement at age 30, 40, or 50-plus to adopt new technologies, or learn new skills in order to be viable in a changed economy and thus remain employed.

Nationally, public and private providers of workforce education and training have been uneven and, in some cases, unresponsive with regard to the quality and diversity of their education and training provisions, thereby contributing to at-risk workers getting even further behind. By contrast, since the late 1970s, San Diego's publicly funded Workforce Investment Board, its community colleges, and extension services and universities have been engaged with the innovators and entrepreneurs who are creating the new economy. They have not just focused on the established trades and businesses that are sustaining the existing economy. The result has been a consistently lower unemployment rate compared to the rest of the state or the nation since the 1990s, jobs and wage growth in the region (until the recent recession where growth has lessened), and an increase in the number of regionally educated college and graduate students able to secure employment in the area. How have they done this?

It is important to underscore, once again, that the San Diego region has not had a history of large, dominant agricultural interests or industrial companies. The closest it came to building a large industrial sector was the defense-contracting clusters that expanded significantly during World War II. Within the defense sector, there were some important dominant employers, such as Convair in aerospace manufacturing. However, as a government contractor with what turned out to be only a short history in the San Diego region, the impact of Convair, while significant, was not as profound as have rivaled the effects of companies such as Kodak in upstate New York, General Motors in central Michigan, or U.S. Steel in Pennsylvania.

Thus, San Diego's workforce has not been overly concentrated in one or two sectors, and San Diego has never been a company town. By the mid-1980s, when the research institutions were getting significant traction, and the community had committed to a technology-commercialization focus through its support of CONNECT, there was a simultaneous focus on job training and retraining. This was not solely because of the commitment to growing innovative enterprises. It was primarily driven by downturns in the real-estate market that affected the construction trades in the region, scandals and bankruptcies in the savings and loan industry that affected jobs in the finance sector, and the early stages of downsizing in defense contracting in response to the end of the Cold War and diminished federal investment in defense manufacturing. All of these factors converged to yield an unemployment rate of more than 10 percent in the San Diego region by the late 1980s. At that time, educators, business leaders, and economic developers were all focused on where new jobs would come from and saw in the burgeoning technology-based business sectors, potential opportunities for displaced workers from industries such as defense manufacturing, engineering and design, finance, and management. During that period, institutional rivalries and local politics were put aside and a network of overlapping leadership from economic development, workforce development, and community-college and university institutions in the region came together in order to identify what role each could play in managing the defense conversion and reemployment process.

By the late 1980s, the CONNECT program had secured a grant to help displaced engineers, managers, and technical professionals identify opportunities in emerging-technology companies and create new start-ups in order to become suppliers and service companies in these growing sectors. The San Diego Community College District had secured funding to implement programs for unemployed production and technical workers in advanced technology, manufacturing, and support activities relevant to the new and emerging technologies in the region. UC San Diego's Extension division, which was already well connected to the growing research-based clusters in the region, launched major further-education programs in CDMA, a new wireless platform being utilized by young companies such as Qualcomm, which today is a standard in the field; courses in clinical research and clinical trials management for the emerging life-sciences companies that were doing Phase I and II clinical trials; and certificate programs in such areas as drug development and biotechnology manufacturing, responsive to the needs of the incubating drug-development companies in the region. The late 1980s and early 1990s saw a proliferation of these sorts of programs among the educational providers in the region. By the mid-to-late 1990s, universities such as San Diego State, UC San Diego, and the University of San Diego were creating degree programs directly relevant to the skills and competencies needed in fields such as wireless communications, drug development, biotech manufacturing, and global science-based business development and management. The number of individuals, educated and certified through these programs is quite impressive. UC San Diego Extension alone has credentialed more than fifteen thousand individuals for careers in these emerging-technology arenas. Additionally, the Extension program at UC San Diego has run an executive program for scientists and engineers over the last twenty-five years, from which more than one thousand senior technology managers in regional science-based companies have graduated.

The publicly funded Workforce Investment Board (WIB) was peripherally involved in many of these initiatives as early as the mid-1980s because of its involvement with defense conversion. However, it is only in the last five to six years that the Workforce Investment Board has begun to be a major player in identifying the wide range of reemployment and new-employment options available to San Diego citizens as a result of the research and development going on in arenas such as health IT, pharmaceuticals, renewables, and clean tech. Additionally, in 2008, a consortium of local foundations came together with the Workforce Investment Board to substantially enlarge the pool of funds available for summer youth-work programs, many of which provided opportunities for inner-city youth to work in new and high-tech companies in the region. In addition, over the last decade, there has been expanded private-sector support for developing entrepreneurship skills among youths, college students, and young adults. In the San Diego region, the business schools today have substantial components of their curriculum focused on building entrepreneurial science-based companies. Within the community, programs such as Junior Achievement and the Downtown Rotary's Camp Enterprise are helping to grow the pipeline of future entrepreneurs.

The phenomenal growth of science and technology school programs across the region—especially of charter schools—has been another important development that relates to the pipeline for talent in science and technology. These programs ensure that low-income and underserved communities have access to the skills, knowledge, and opportunities for employment that more privileged middle- and upper-middle-class children have. Two of the nation's top-ten high schools, as reported by *Newsweek*[191] are both young "fast-track" charter schools, founded in San Diego less than fifteen years ago, with curricular emphasis on science and technology. Both schools select students from lotteries and represent low-income and new-immigrant children whose parents did not attend college. Today, as many as 90 percent of their graduates move into university-level education as well as technical careers. The Preuss School on the UC San Diego campus and High Tech High, which began with one campus and now has twelve campuses across the region, are stunning examples of how the community has mobilized to support innovative educational provisions that will enhance the skills and competencies of previously under-represented groups in science and technology fields.

In addition, the Girard Foundation, whose philanthropic corpus was established by a successful technology entrepreneur, has invested over twenty years in innovative uses of technology in public-school classrooms and the founding of innovative charter schools across the region. Athena, a group of women entrepreneurs and science-based business support professionals, which numbers more than five hundred women, annually gives college scholarships to young women going into university careers in science and technology. Achievement Rewards for College Scientists (ARCS) is another volunteer fund-raising group which supports annual scholarships for as many as fifty students in university science and technology fields. Finally, the University of California has a number of summer institutes and camps focused on introducing middle school and high school students to the opportunities in science and technology, most notable of which are COSMOS and Academic Connections.

What these brief examples are meant to demonstrate is that local communities can organize their education and training institutions to be active partners in the a) development of the K¬–12 pipeline for science and technology jobs, b) provision of college and university programs that provide people with the fundamental skills they need, and c) assurance that programs exist for retraining and upgrading technical skills and that robust lifelong learning is available for college graduates in science and technology fields.

More than twenty years ago, San Diego began developing curricula targeted to the needs of the regional economy in a collaborative and complementary manner. The overlapping, boundary-spanning networks were developed in the face of an economic crisis of the 1980s. In the absence of legacy industries, such as automobile manufacturing, that people waited to "come back," San Diego was forced to look forward—not backward. The result is an economic environment that is not only continuously innovative with regard to companies, but is continuously renewing with regard to workforce. UC San Diego, one of the nation's preeminent research institutions and its Extension division, animated by its land-grant university heritage, has driven much of the innovation in workforce education and training for the region. However, the actual provision of education and training has been distributed across a wide array of regional institutions, on whose boards technology entrepreneurs as well as traditional industry leaders sit. There are valuable principles of practice to be derived from San Diego's experience of retooling and refocusing its regional workforce so that innovation, job development, and job creation could happen simultaneously.

The lessons from San Diego are clear. For communities nationwide to better integrate innovation with job development and creation, they must make a major commitment to continuous education and training (lifelong learning).[192] Our postmodern world is characterized by perpetual change and uncertainty. Individuals, organizations, and communities must continually adapt; shed old practices and structures; and integrate new information, skills, and systems to accomplish the desired goals at home, at work, and in the community. That is the imperative of living in a knowledge age. We have to recognize that learning throughout life is the only way to manage or adapt to change.

This continuous change is driven by many factors, but to reiterate, it can be broadly understood in terms of three macro-phenomena which touch all communities: rapid technological change, massive demographic shifts, and globalization—the very same forces driving innovation.

The forces of technology are everywhere, not just in the reported new economy of dot coms, biosciences, composite materials, and bioinformatics. However, as we discussed earlier, advances in science and technology result not only in new products and industries; they transform traditional ones. Agricultural food processing becomes as important as food production. Computer design and cutting equipment change clothing and furniture manufacturing. Super-computer–simulated earthquakes, drug testing, prosthetic-device assessments change how research explores complex questions previously requiring natural settings. And so, regardless of our initial level of educational attainment, the content of our lives and work is continuously shifting and we must learn new things.

The forces of demographic change go far beyond the usual indicators of population concentration in urban centers throughout Europe and

America, or the growing number of elderly as a particular percentage of our population. The challenging implications lie in such facts as, for example, 11 percent of the two million residents of the City of San Diego is Filipino and 6 percent is African American; or that, today, in the United States, there are more Muslims than Jews and more Buddhists than Episcopalians. Also, more Americans work for companies owned by women than they do for Fortune 500 companies. These demographic trends speak volumes about what one has to "know"—sometimes unlearn, always relearn—in order to effectively develop management and leadership skills; design, manufacture, and sell products; teach children; treat patients; run successful cinemas, bookstores, or arts and cultural organizations.

Finally, globalization—the fact that ideas, investment capital, manufacturing and distribution centers, suppliers, and markets are no longer concentrated exclusively in a few major cities, but are present, accessible, and mobile across the globe—means that local communities, regional suppliers and producers, and consumers everywhere are as affected by developments in London or Hong Kong as they are by developments in Washington, D.C. or their own state capital. Regardless of locale, it is possible to participate in global enterprise or be undermined by a competitor from abroad.

The force of these factors—technology, demography, and globalization—also gives rise to a paradox of modern times that is essential to grasp when thinking about connecting education and training to innovation outcomes: "Think globally, act locally." Everything local is affected by macro trends, often driven by developments outside one's region, and yet the only way to understand, harness, shape, and integrate these forces into our civic and work lives is through local and regional initiatives. These initiatives must support continuous learning and facilitate the integration of new knowledge and skills into the daily activities of individuals, organizations, and communities in their regions. That is why citizens, industry leaders, politicians, and "do-gooders" everywhere are calling upon community colleges and universities to become more engaged in regional development. Today, university engagement means not just producing the research and scholarship that is shaping the macro drivers of economies or the initial credentialing of the intellectual and human capital, but contributing to the economy and society. A new form of engagement is essential. This form of engagement acknowledges that, increasingly, the key users of knowledge are regionally based.

Thus, it requires a distinctively regional approach to meeting the life-long learning needs of local industries, both established and emerging. The ongoing interactions between the leaders of the innovation community and the leaders of the education and training communities, such as one finds in locales like San Diego, significantly improve the possibility of a region's experiencing broad workforce benefits from its innovation economy. It also assures that individuals pursuing their education, seeking jobs, building or changing their careers have the most timely information available about where the job opportunities are and what knowledge and skills will be required. And finally, it means that the workforce has access to the entrepreneurs and principals in the new and high-growth companies.

These lessons from San Diego illustrate the importance of ongoing linkages with all the key players. Any region serious about innovation and job creation should strive to create platforms that regularly bring together the four key players: the research community, the entrepreneurs and investors, the economic developers, and the educators and workforce-training organizations. This is the only way to close America's job gap.

ABOUT THE AUTHORS

Mary Walshok, Ph.D., is an author, educator, job-creation expert, dean of University Extension, and associate vice chancellor for public programs at the University of California, San Diego. She is a thought leader and subject-matter expert on employability, career reinvention, and the new innovation economy.

As an industrial social scientist studying the dynamics of regional economic growth and transformation, Walshok has been pleasantly surprised by her visits to communities across America that most people rarely think of as pockets of innovation and transformation. Many of these regions take advantage of federal stimulus funds; some are simply organizing at the regional level to repurpose their existing industrial and commercial capabilities, reskill their workforce, and restore their previously innovative and entrepreneurial know-how.

Walshok has authored numerous book chapters and articles on the world of work, including, *Blue Collar Women* and *Knowledge Without Boundaries: What America's Research Universities Can Do for the Economy, the Workplace, and the Community.*

She is the author of more than one hundred articles and reports on regional innovation, the role of research institutions in regional economies, and workforce development, including the forthcoming book with Stanford University Press, *Invention and Reinvention: The Evolution of San Diego's Entrepreneurial Economy.* She is currently leading comparative research projects on regional innovation outcomes funded by NSF and NIH.

As head of the continuing-education and public-programs arm of UC San Diego for nearly three decades, Walshok oversees programs that educate approximately 54,000 enrollees annually, which translates to more than 22,600 students in over 4,600 courses. Walshok has developed outreach efforts to help accelerate the San Diego region's economic vitality, assure a globally competitive talent pool, and help college graduates transition to employment areas that are in hot-growth fields.

During her tenure she has played an active part in helping the University expand its local impact, national reputation, and global reach. UC San Diego, one of the ten campuses in the world-renowned University of California system, has rapidly achieved its status as one of the top fifty institutions in the world for higher education and research.

Tapan Munroe, Ph.D., is a recognized author, speaker, consultant, and advisor in economics. His expertise includes regional economics, environmental economics, and high-tech industry analysis. His current research and writings focus on the economics of innovation and economies of Silicon Valley and the Bay Area and other high-tech regions.

Tapan Munroe has authored three books relating to Silicon Valley: *Dot-Com to Dot-Bomb: Understating the Dot-Com Boom, Bust and Resurgence*, Moraga Press, 2004; *Silicon Valley: The Ecology of Innovation*, Science Parks Association of Spain, 2008; and *What Makes Silicon Valley Tick?*, Nova Vista Publishing, 2009. He has been a columnist on economic issues for the *San Francisco Examiner* and the *Journal of Corporate Renewal*. He is also a columnist for several MediaNews Group newspapers, including the *Oakland Tribune* and the *Contra Costa Times*. He is a commentator on both regional and national radio and TV news programs including KRON-4 TV, KGO-7 TV, CNBC in Los Angeles and New York, the Dow Jones Investors Network, and the Bloomberg News Service.

He is a member of the Advisory Board of City National Bank in San Francisco; a member-investor with the Keiretsu Forum, the nation's largest business angel-investment organization; emeritus member of the Board of Directors of the Center for Pacific Rim Studies at the University of San Francisco; and a member of the University of California President's

Board on Science and Innovation. He has also served as a trustee of the UC Merced Foundation.

Munroe has been a director of LECG, LLC, a worldwide consulting firm and currently serves as an affiliate. He served as the chief economist for Pacific Gas and Electric Company for more than a decade. He is also a former president of the National Association of Business Economists, Bay Area Chapter; a former member of the National Petroleum Council Task Force on Oil Prices; former quarterly chair for the Commonwealth Club of California; and the former chair of the Economics Committee for Edison Electric in Washington, D.C.

Tapan holds a Ph.D. in economics from the University of Colorado where he was awarded a fellowship and membership in Phi Kappa Phi and Omicron Delta Epsilon. He is also a graduate of the University of Chicago Executive Training Program; a visiting scholar at the Massachusetts Institute of Technology, Stanford University, and the University of Augsburg in West Germany; an adjunct professor at the University of California, Berkeley; and a professor and chair for the Department of Economics at the University of the Pacific in Stockton. From 1998 to 1999, he was the holder of the Kiriyama Distinguished Professorship for Asia Pacific Studies at the University of San Francisco.

Henry DeVries, MBA, is a job and career expert who speaks to thousands of business owners and executives each year, teaching them how to grow their businesses and advance their careers. As assistant dean, he has helped the continuing education arm of University of California, San Diego, grow enrollments in certificate programs by 44 percent in three years. He is responsible for communications for 4,600 Extension classes that annually attract 54,000 people interested in career advancement. In addition, he is the "Jobs and Careers" section editor of the online news magazine *San Diego News Network* and the "Jobs and Careers" columnist for *San Diego Metropolitan* magazine.

Along with his books *Self-Marketing Secrets* and *Pain Killer Marketing*, the tools of DeVries have been used to dramatically advance careers and increase revenue for businesses for more than a decade. He has teaching appointments at three California universities and has taught marketing to entrepreneurs at Columbia University and at many national conferences.

Prior to founding his own company, the New Client Marketing Institute, he used his systems to generate more than 100,000 qualified leads a year for a $5 billion financial-services organization and was president of an advertising agency where his systems helped double billings and land the firm in the Ad Age 500. His clients ranged from Fortune 500, Inc., 500 and billion-dollar corporations listed on the New York Stock Exchange to professional sports teams and nonprofit organizations.

He is an award-winning member of the Public Relations Society of America and earned the group's APR accreditation in 1994. A former president of the UC San Diego Alumni Association, DeVries earned his BA at UC San Diego and his MBA from San Diego State University, and completed specialized training at Harvard Business School. An award-winning writer, he is the author of seventeen business books (five under his name, twelve that he penned for others) and has taught marketing at UC San Diego since 1984.

ENDNOTES

[1] Friedman, Thomas L.,Start-Ups, Not Bailouts, The New York Times, April 4, 2010.

[2] Reports: Rising Above the Gathering Storm: Energizing and Employing America for a Brighter Economic Future (The National Academic Press, 2007); Rising Above the Gathering Storm Two Years Later: Accelerating Progress Toward a Brighter Economic Future (The National Academic Press, 2009); Knowledge Retention and Transfer in the World of Work (Manpower, 2010).

[3] ASTD Reports: The State of the Industry Report 2009, Learning in Tough Economic Times, August 2009.

[4] Adams, James Truslow, The Epic of America, 1931.

[5] Kotkin, Joel, Tribes. (Random House, 1994).

[6] "A Special Report on the American Economy", The Economist, April 3, 2010.

[7] The Economist, op. cit.

[8] Florida, Richard, "How the Crash Will Reshape America", The Atlantic magazine, March 2009.

[9] Choma,Russ, Renewable Energy Money Still Going Abroad, Despite Criticism From Congress, American University School of Communication, Investigative Reporting Workshop, February, 2010.

[10] Jones, Van, The Green Collar Economy: How One Solution Can Fix Our Two Biggest Problems, (HarperOne, 2009), page 14.

[11] Ibid, page 15.

[12] Ibid, page 15.

[13] Ibid, page 16.

[14] Ibid, page 17-18.

[15] Stangler, Dane and Litan, Robert E., Where Will The Jobs Come From?, Kauffman Foundation Research Series: Firm Foundation and Economic Growth, November 2009.

[16] BLS, Occupational Outlook Quarterly, Winter 2009-10.

[17] Carnevale, Anthony P., Smith, Nicole, Strohl, Jeff, Help Wanted: Projections of Jobs and Education Requirements Through 2018, Center on Education and the Workforce, Georgetown University, June 2010.

[18] Munroe, Tapan, Bay Area News Group column, March 18, 2010.

[19] ASTD Report, Bridging the Skills Gap: New Factors Compound the Growing Skills Shortage, Alexandria, Virginia, 2009.

[20] Davenport, Thomas, Thinking for a Living, (Harvard Business School Press, 2005).

[21] ASTD report, p.5, op cit.

[22] Munroe, Tapan, Bay Area News Group column, March 18, 2010.

[23] ASTD 2009 report, p.4,op cit.

[24] Munroe, Tapan, Bay Area News Group column, April 4, 2010.

[25] Munroe, Tapan, Bay Area News Group column, April 1, 2010.

[26] Ibid.

[27] Munroe, Tapan, Bay Area News Group column, April 15, 2010.

[28] Gordon, Edward E., Winning the Global Talent Showdown (Barrett-Koehler Publishers, San Francisco, 2009).

[29] Levy, Frank & Murname, Richard J., The New Dimension of Labor: How Computers are creating the Next Job Market, Russell Sage Foundation, New York, 2004.

[30] Gordon, Edward E. op. cit., p.8.

[31] Munroe, Tapan, Bay Area News Group column, January 21, 2009.

[32] Caron, S., Nov.11, 2008, www.insidesrm.com

[33] Schramm, Carl, Litan, Robert and Stangler, Dane New Business, Not Small Business, Is What Creates Jobs, The *Wall Street Journal*, November 6, 2009.

[34] Anthony, Scott, Innovation During the Great Disruption, Forbes.com, Jan. 18, 2009.

[35] Munroe, Tapan, Bay Area News Group column, January 21, 2009.

[36] UC San Diego Extension Report: Hot Careers for College Graduates 2010, www.extension.UC San Diego.edu

[37] Inheriting a Complex World: Future Leaders Envision Sharing the Planet, IBM Institute for Business Value, June 2010.

[38] Manpower Inc. Warns Global Skilled Trades Shortage Could Stall Future Economic Growth, http://press.manpower.com, August 25, 2010

[39] The Global Competitiveness Report 2009-2010, Table 5.08 Extent of Staff Training, World Economic Forum, 2009.

[40] Hughes, Kathleen, Employment: Employers' Perceptions of Employment Readiness, www.answers.com (8/24/2010).

[41] Highlights from PISA 2006: Performance of U.S. 15-Year-Old Students in Science and Mathematics Literacy in an International Context, Organization for Cooperation and Development December 2007.

[42] Report: State of Metropolitan America – on the Front Lines of Demographic Transformation, Metropolitan Policy Programs at Brookings, May 2010.

[43] The Economist, A Special Report on Innovation in Emerging Markets, April 17, 2010.

[44] Occupational Outlook Handbook, 2010-11 Edition, U.S. Department of Labor Bureau of Labor Statistics <http://www.bls.gov/oco/ocos064.htm>, accessed on March 22, 2010.

[45] Guide to College Majors in Health Information Technology, www.WorldWide-Learn.com, www.worldwidelearn.com, accessed March 24, 2010.

[46] Ibid.

[47] Author Unknown, http://www.medpac.gov/publications/congressional_reports/June04_ch7.pdf, access March 24, 2010.

[48] DeVries, Henry, Recovery Training Funds Available for Health care IT Jobs, UC SAN DIEGO News, http://UC San Diegonews.UC San Diego.edu/newsrel/general/07-09ARRA.asp (July 29, 2009).

[49] Bureau of Labor Statistics, op cit.

[50] DeVries, Henry, op cit.

[51] Ibid.

[52] Arlington, Steve and Farino, Anthony, Biomarket Trends: Pharmaceutical Industry Undergoing Transformation, Genetic Engineering & Biotechnology News, Vol. 27, No. 15 (Sep 1, 2007).

[53] Steve Arlington, op cit.

[54] Ibid.

[55] Drug Approvals – From Invention to Market…A 12-Year Trip, MedicineNet.com, < http://www.medicinenet.com/script/main/art.asp?articlekey=9877, (July 14, 1999).

[56] Arlington, Steve and Farino, Anthony, op cit.

[57] "Clinical Trials," in American Statistical Association, <http://www.amstat.org/careers/clinicaltrials.cfm>, accessed March 23, 2010.

[58] "Challenges in Oncology Clinical Trial Design," in Decision Resources, Inc., <http://www.researchandmarkets.com/reports/452451>, (March 2007).

[59] "Challenges in Oncology Clinical Trial Design," op cit.

[60] Ibid.

[61] Thearling, Kurt, Ph.D., An Introduction to Data Mining, http://www.thearling.com/text/dmwhite/dmwhite.htm, accessed March 25, 2010.

[62] "Data Mining," in Exforsys Inc, <http://www.exforsys.com/tutorials/data-mining.html>, accessed March 25, 2010.

[63] Thearling, Kurt, op cit.

[64] Thearling, Kurt, op cit.

[65] Scamman, Karen, Top careers for college graduates: Data Mining, www.Examiner.com, <http://www.examiner.com/x-11055-San-Diego-College-Life-Examiner~y2009m6d4-Top-careers-for-college-graduates-Data-Mining>, (June 4, 2009).

[66] Scamman, Karen, op cit.

[67] Ibid.

[68] Mehradadi, Bruce, Why Study for an Embedded Systems Degree?, Studying Science and Engineering Worldwide, <http://www.science-engineering.net/embedded-systems.htm >, accessed March 28, 2010.

[69] Embedded Systems Engineering Technology, Oregon Institute of Technology, <http://www.oit.edu/programs/klamath-falls/computer-systems-engineering-technology/embedded-systems-engineering-technology/overview>, accessed March 28, 2010.

[70] Mehradadi, Bruce, op cit.

[71] Occupational Outlook Handbook, 2010-11 Edition, U.S. Department of Labor Bureau of Labor Statistics < http://www.bls.gov/oco/ocos304.htm>, accessed on March 28, 2010.

[72] Occupational Outlook Handbook, op cit.

[73] 2009 Digital Future Report, Center for the Digital Future, University of Southern California, USC Annenberg School for Communication & Journalism, <http://www.digitalcenter.org/pages/current_report.asp?intGlobalId=43>, (April 28, 2009).

[74] 2009 Digital Future Report, op cit.

[75] Varnelis, Kazys, Networked Publics, in www.NetworkedPublics.org, <http://networkedpublics.org/>, (MIT Press, 2008).

[76] Moor, Anthony, Go to the Web, Young Journalist, in Online Journalism Review, (March 16, 2006).

[77] Hernandez, Robert, Wanted: Required Journalism Skills, Online Journalism Review, Knight Digital Media Center, USC Annenberg School for Communication & Journalism, (Feb. 9, 2010).

[78] Journalism Career Requirements, in www.CareerRequirement.com, <www.careerrequirement.com >, accessed, March 28, 2010.

[79] Niles, Robert, Keeping Your Job in Journalism, Online Journalism Review, (March 5, 2008).

[80] Niles, Robert, op cit.

[81] Industry Trends Point to Unprecedented Opportunities, Interim Health care, <http://www.interimhealth care.com/franchise/info/industry_trends.aspx>, accessed March 28, 2010.

[82] Trends in The Elderly Population, Aging in the Know, <http://www.healthinaging.org/agingintheknow/chapters_ch_trial.asp?ch=2#Increasing>, accessed March 28, 2010.

[83] Industry Trends Point to Unprecedented Opportunities, op cit.

[84] U.S. Census Bureau Public Information Office, Census Bureau Projects Doubling Of Nation's Population By 2050, United States Department of Commerce News, < http://www.census.gov/Press-Release/www/2000/cb00-05.html>, (January 13, 2000).

[85] Plunkett Research, U.S. Health care Industry Overview, Plunket Research Ltd., <http://www.plunkettresearch.com/Industries/Health care/Health careStatistics/tabid/293/Default.aspx>, accessed March 28, 2010.

[86] Industry Trends Point to Unprecedented Opportunities, op cit.

[87] Ibid.

[88] Ibid.

[89] Health in Aging Stories, in The AGS Foundation for Health in Aging, < http://www.healthinaging.org/caregiver/geriatric.asp>, accessed March 28, 2010.

[90] Trends in The Elderly Population, op cit.

[91] Ibid.

[92] Howard, Jacqueline, What's coming next in online news? , OJR: The Online Journalism Review   http://www.ojr.org/ojr/people/JacquelineHoward/201003/1834/ (March 23, 2010).

[93] Ibid.

[94] Occupational Outlook Handbook, 2010-11 Edition, U.S. Department of Labor Bureau of Labor Statistics < http://www.bls.gov/oco/ocos303.htm >, accessed on March 22, 2010.

[95] O'Brien,Chris, Mobilizing for Mobile: Are news organizations lagging?, News Leadership 3.0, Knight Digital Media Center, < Mobilizing for mobile: Are news organizations lagging?> , (August 24, 2009).

[96] Ibid.

[97] Ibid.

[98] Ibid.

[99] How Internet and Cell Phone Users Have Turned News into a Social Experience, Journalism.org, Pew Research Center's Project for Excellence in Journalism,   http://www.journalism.org/analysis_report/understanding_participatory_news_consumer >, (March 01, 2010).

[100] O'Brien, Chris, op cit.

[101] Occupational Health and Safety Specialists, Occupation Profile, America's Career Infonet, > http://www.acinet.org/acinet/occ_rep.asp?level=&optstatus=11111 1111&id=,8&nodeid=2&soccode=299011&stfips=10>, accessed March 28, 2010.

[102] Ibid.

[103] Ibid.

[104] Occupational and Environmental Epidemiology, in Environmental Health Sciences, University of Michigan School of Public Health, <http://www.sph.umich.edu/ehs/oee/index.html>, accessed March 28, 2010.

[105] Ibid.

[106] Bureau of Labor Statistics Occupational Outlook Handbook 2010-11, op cit.

[107] Occupational Health and Safety Specialists, op cit.

[108] Spanish, Encyclopedia Britannica eb.com, <http://www.britannica.com/EBchecked/topic/558113/Spanish-language>, accessed on April 2, 2010.

[109] Spanish Language, Trusted Translations, < http://www.trustedtranslations.com/spanish-language>, accessed April 3, 2010.

[110] Occupational Outlook Handbook, 2010-11 Edition, op cit.

[111] Spanish, op cit.

[112] Occupational Outlook Handbook, 2010-11 Edition, op cit

[113] Spanish, op cit.

[114] Occupational Outlook Handbook, 2010-11 Edition, op cit.

[115] Ibid.

[116] Ibid.

[117] Ibid.

[118] DeVries, Henry. Get Them While They're Hot; Study Reveals One Dozen Hot Career Trends, UC San Diego Extension, <http://extension.UC San Diego.edu/Student/images/careerTrends.pdf>, accessed March 25, 2010.

[119] Green Jobs Overview, JobMonkey.com, <http://www.jobmonkey.com/green-jobs/>, accessed March 26, 2010.

[120] What is LEED? , LEED Rating Systems, U.S. Green Building Council, <http://www.usgbc.org/DisplayPage.aspx?CMSPageID=222>, accessed March 27, 2010.

[121] The Engaged Organization; Corporate Employee Environmental Education-Survey and Case Study Findings, National Environmental Education Foundation, http://www.neefusa.org/BusinessEnv/EngagedOrganization_03182009.pdf (March 2009).

[122] 25 Big Companies that are Going Green, Business Pundit, <http://www.businesspundit.com/25-big-companies-that-are-going-green/> (July 29, 2008).

[123] Szaky, Tom, Do Green Companies Need Green Employees?, TriplePundit. com, <http://www.triplepundit.com/2008/09/tom-szaky-do-green-companies-need-green-employees/>, (September 25, 2010).

[124] The Engaged Organization; Corporate Employee Environmental Education Survey and Case Study Findings, op cit.

[125] Hildebrand, Deborah S., The Greening of the American Workforce; The Importance of Eco-Friendly Employees in Today's Job Market, Suite101.com, <http://careerplanning.suite101.com/article.cfm/the_greening_of_the_american_workforce> , (July 29, 2009).

[126] Team Treehugger, How to Go Green: At Work, PlanetGreen.com, <http://planetgreen.discovery.com/go-green/green-work/>, accessed March 25, 2010.

[127] Occupational Outlook Handbook, 2010-11 Edition, U.S. Department of Labor Bureau of Labor Statistics <http://www.bls.gov/oco/ocos064.htm>, accessed on April 3, 2010.

[128] Occupational Outlook Handbook, 2010-11 Edition, op cit.

[129] Ibid.

[130] Ibid.

[131] Occupational Outlook Handbook, 2010-11 Edition, U.S. Department of Labor Bureau of Labor Statistics <http://www.bls.gov/oco/ocos289.htm>, accessed on April 6, 2010.

[132] Occupational Outlook Handbook, 2010-11 Edition, op cit.

[133] Beare, Kenneth, Before You Decide to Become an ESL Teacher, <http://esl.about.com/od/esleflteachertraining/bb/bydecidetefl.htm>, accessed on April 6, 2010.

[134] Ibid.

[135] UC San Diego General Catalog 2009-2010, <http://www.UC San Diego.edu/catalog/curric/MBC.html>, accessed on April 7, 2010.

[136] Jackson, Jeremy, (Scripps Institution of Oceanography at UC San Diego), Beyond the Obituaries: Successful Fish Stories in Ocean Conservation, speech given at the 2009 American Association for the Advancement of Science (AAAS) meeting, Chicago, Illinois, February 13, 2009. <http://scrippsnews.UC San Diego.edu/Releases/?releaseID=961>, accessed on April 7, 2010.

[137] Ibid.

[138] Cali Turner Tomaszewicz, personal interview, June 2, 2009, <http://mbc.UC San Diego.edu/people/bio-student-Turner.cfm>, accessed on April 7, 2010.

[139] Ahearn, Dan (Attorney Adviser), Health care Law: A Career Guide, President and Fellows of Harvard College, 2004, p. 4, <http://www.law.harvard.edu/current/careers/opia/planning/career-resources/docs/guide-health-law.pdf>, accessed on April 7, 2010.

[140] Occupational Outlook Handbook, 2010-11 Edition, U.S. Department of Labor Bureau of Labor Statistics < http://www.bls.gov/oco/ocos066.htm>, accessed on April 6, 2010.

[141] Shook, Ray, Welding has a new spark, Welding &Gases Today Online, <http://www.weldingandgasestoday.org/content/1q10/weldingtrends.php> accessed on May 3, 2010.

[142] Ibid.

[143] Ibid.

[144] Liao, Janet and Ladika, Susan, Got Welding Skills? Experienced welders are in high demand—and hard to find, Forward Online, <http://forward.msci.org/articles/1107got-welding-skills.cfm#>, accessed on May 7, 2010.

[145] Occupational Outlook Handbook, 2010-11 Edition, U.S. Department of Labor Bureau of Labor Statistics <http://www.bls.gov/oco/ocos226.htm>, accessed on May 7, 2010.

[146] American Welding Society, www.aws.org http://www.aws.org/w/sense/, accessed on May 7, 2010.

[147] Ibid.

[148] Heston, Tim, Ernest Levert: Fabricating Equipment News Welder of the Year, Metal Forming and Fabricating, <http://www.fandmmag.com/online/article.jsp?id=295&siteSection=2>, accessed on May 7, 2010.

[149] Employee Attendance Problems Drag Down the Profits, Creative Business Resources, 2010.

[150] Basu & Weibull, Punctuality: A Cultural Trait as Equilibrium, Social Science Research Network, June 10, 2002.

[151] Wescott, Bidding Adios to 'Manana', BBC News, March 1, 2007.

[152] Surowjecki, James, Punctuality Pays, The New Yorker, April 5, 2004.

[153] Report: State of Metropolitan America – on the Front Lines of Demographic Transformation, Metropolitan Policy Programs at Brookings, May 2010.

[154] An earlier version of this discussion appears in a chapter by Walshok Mary L. and Lee, Caroline W. B. in the forthcoming book edited by O'Shea R.P. & Allen TJ, Building Technology Transfer in Research Universities: An Entrepreneurial Approach, Cambridge University Press.

[155] Anderson, Nancy Scott, An Improbable Venture: A History of the University of California, San Diego, (UC SAN DIEGO Press, 1993, pp. 26, 52-65). This work constitutes an official history of UC SAN DIEGO from 1900 to 1993.

[156] Ibid, p. 71.

[157] Walshok, Mary L., Connecting Science and Business, Chapter 9 in Miller, Robert C., Le Boeuf, Bernard J. et al Developing University-Industry Relations: Pathways to Innovation from the West Coast, (Jossey-Bass, 2009).

[158] CONNECT Spring 2010 San Diego Innovation Report.

[159] Homans, George, Social Behavior: Its Elementary Forms, 1974.

[160] CONNECT Spring 2010 San Diego Innovation Report.

[161] Miller, Robert C., Le Boeuf, Bernard J., Nine Principles for Successful University-Industry Relations, Chapter 10 in Miller, Robert C., Le Boeuf, Bernard J. et al Developing University-Industry Relations: Pathways to Innovation from the West Coast, (Jossey-Bass, 2009).

[162] Florida, Richard, Who's Your City? (Basic Books, 2008).

[163] Mills, Karen G., Reynolds, Elizabeth B., Reamer, Andrew, Clusters and Competitiveness: A New Federal Role for Stimulating Regional Economies (The Brooking Institution, April 2008).

[164] The New Face of Higher Education: Lifelong Learning Trends, University Continuing Education, p.54, 2009.

[165] Lohrentz, Tim, Review and Analysis of the Literature: The Business Benefits of Employee Development, National Network of Sector Partners (March 15, 2010).

[166] Ahlstrand, Amanda L., Bassi, Laurie J. and McMurrer, Daniel P., Workplace Education for Low-Wage Workers, W.E. Upjohn Institute for Employment Research, Kalamazoo, MI (2003).

[167] Bassi, Laurie and McMurrer, Daniel, Are Skills a Cost or Asset? The Milken Institute Review, (Quarter 3, 2004).

[168] Coy, Peter, Help Wanted: Why That Sign's Bad, Businessweek, April 9, 2009.

[169] The Pros and Cons of Providing Employee Continuing Education, HR World, August 8, 2008.

[170] Fraziz, Harley and Speltzer. James R., Worker training: what we have learned from the NLSY79, Monthly Labor Review, February 2005.

[171] Bloom, Michael R. and Lafleur, Brenda, Turning Skills into Profit: Economic Benefits of Workplace Education Program, The Conference Board, 1999.

[172] Conway, Maureen, Blair, Amy Kays, Gibbons, Catherine, Investigating Demand Side Outcomes: Literature Review and Implications, the Aspen Institute, March 2003.

[173] Hollenbeck, Kevin, Is there a Role for Public Support of Incumbent Worker On-the-Job Training?, Upjohn Institute Staff Working Paper No. 08-138, January 2008.

[174] Review of Information on the Benefits of Training for Employers, Department for Business and Information Skills, United Kingdom, June 3, 1997.

[175] T. Hoerner, Further Education for current employees: Smart employer policy?, www.helium.com (accessed June 17, 2010).

[176] The New Face of Higher Education: Lifelong Learning Trends, University Continuing Education, p.54, 2009.

[177] Ibid, p.55.

[178] AARP report, Employment at Older Ages and the Changing Nature of Work, November 2007.

[179] Munroe, Tapan, Oakland Tribune, November 22, 2009.

[180] Caron, S., Nov.11, 2008, www.insidesrm.com

[181] Munroe, Tapan, Oakland Tribune, January 31, 2010.

[182] Wulf, William A., Changes in Innovation Ecology, Science, Vol. 316, No. 5829, p.1253, June 1, 2007.

[183] In this connection it is important to review the following books: James. F.Moore, The Death of Competition: Leadership and Strategy in the Age of Business Ecosystems (Harper Business, 1996); Marco Iansiti and Roy Levien, The Keystone Advantage: What the Dynamics of Business Ecosystems Mean for Strategy, Innovation, and Sustainability (Harvard Business School Press, 2004).

[184] Munroe, T. and Westwind, M., What Makes Silicon Valley Tick? (Nova Vista Publishing, 2009).

[185] "Entrepreneurship is the process of identifying, developing, and bringing a vision to life. The vision may be an innovative idea, an opportunity, more simply a better way of doing something. The end result is the creation of a new venture, formed under conditions of risk and considerable uncertainty." The Entrepreneurship Center at Miami University of Ohio.

[186] Ibid, pp. 98-101.

[187] Chong-Moon Lee, et al, The Silicon Valley Edge: A Habitat for Innovation and Entrepreneurship (Stanford University Press, 2000).

[188] Center for Venture Research, University of New Hampshire.

[189] http://nvca.org/def.html

[190] Audretsch, David B. and Thurik, A. Roy, What's New about the New Economy,

Industrial and Corporate Change, Vol. 10, No 1, pp. 267-315 (Oxford University Press, 2001).

[191] America's Top Public High Schools, *Newsweek*, May 2, 2010

[192] Walshok, Mary L., Facilitating Lifelong learning in a Research University Context, Chapter 12 in Hirsch, Werner Z. and Weber, Luc E., As the Walls of Academia are Tumbling Down, (Economica, 2002).

INDEX

F

G

K

Kansas City, MO, 46

Kaslow, Amy, 30

Kauffman Foundation, 14, 36

Kellogg Foundation, 115

Kotkin, Joel, 4

Kraft, 35, 149

Krantz, Vicki, 80

Krugman, Paul, 150

L

Le Boeuf, Bernard J., 126

Leadership in Energy and Environmental Design (LEED), 80-81

Leisure and hospitality, 21

Levert, Ernest, 92

Li, Nikki, 68-70

Liang, Brian, 89-90

Linkabit, 109, 114-115

Lockheed Martin Electronic Systems, 92

Lohrentz, Tim, 134

Los Angeles Times, xi

Low-skill industrial jobs, 22, 32

Lux Art Institute, 69

M

M.D. Anderson, 156

MIT, 156, 161

MTV Networks, 35, 149

Machado, Rob, 93

Mackey, Tim, 88-90

Mackinac Bridge, 11-12

Madoff, Bernie, x-xi

Management style, 165-166

N

T

X

Y

THIS BOOK DOESN'T END
AT THE LAST PAGE!

We want to hear from you!

Register your book at:

www.WBusinessBooks.com to receive the latest business news and information.

You can communicate with the author or share your thoughts about this book with other members of the WBusiness community.

www.WBusinessBooks.com is a place where you can sharpen your skills, learn the new trends and network with other professionals.